Clear**Revise**™

AQA GCSE
Computer Science 8525

Illustrated revision and practice

Python Edition

Published by
PG Online Limited
The Old Coach House
35 Main Road
Tolpuddle
Dorset
DT2 7EW
United Kingdom

sales@pgonline.co.uk
www.pgonline.co.uk
2020

PG ONLINE

PREFACE

Absolute clarity! That's the aim.

This is everything you need to ace your exam and beam with pride. Each topic is laid out in a beautifully illustrated format that is clear, approachable and as concise and simple as possible.

Each section of the specification is clearly indicated to help you cross-reference your revision. The checklist on the contents pages will help you keep track of what you have already worked through and what's left before the big day.

We have included worked examination-style questions with answers for almost every topic. This helps you understand where marks are coming from and to see the theory at work for yourself in an examination situation. There is also a set of exam-style questions at the end of each section for you to practise writing answers for. You can check your answers against those given at the end of the book.

A free pack of over 30 Python solutions to accompany each of the programs listed in the book is available to download from pgonline.co.uk.

LEVELS OF LEARNING

Based on the degree to which you are able to truly understand a new topic, we recommend that you work in stages. Start by reading a short explanation of something, then try and recall what you've just read. This has limited effect if you stop there but it aids the next stage. Question everything. Write down your own summary and then complete and mark a related exam-style question. Cover up the answers if necessary, but learn from them once you've seen them. Lastly, teach someone else. Explain the topic in a way that they can understand. Have a go at the different practice questions – they offer an insight into how and where marks are awarded.

ACKNOWLEDGEMENTS

The questions in the ClearRevise textbook are the sole responsibility of the authors and have neither been provided nor approved by the examination board.

Every effort has been made to trace and acknowledge ownership of copyright. The publishers will be happy to make any future amendments with copyright owners that it has not been possible to contact. The publisher would like to thank the following companies and individuals who granted permission for the use of their images in this textbook.

Design and artwork: Jessica Webb / PG Online Ltd
Graphics / images: © Shutterstock

First edition 2020
A catalogue entry for this book is available from the British Library
ISBN: 978-1-910523-25-4
Copyright © PG Online 2020
All rights reserved

Printed on FSC certified paper by Bell and Bain Ltd, Glasgow, UK.

THE SCIENCE OF REVISION

Illustrations and words

Research has shown that revising with words and pictures doubles the quality of responses by students.[1] This is known as 'dual-coding' because it provides two ways of fetching the information from our brain. The improvement in responses is particularly apparent in students when asked to apply their knowledge to different problems. Recall, application and judgement are all specifically and carefully assessed in public examination questions.

Retrieval of information

Retrieval practice encourages students to come up with answers to questions.[2] The closer the question is to one you might see in a real examination, the better. Also, the closer the environment in which a student revises is to the 'examination environment', the better. Students who had a test 2–7 days away did 30% better using retrieval practice than students who simply read, or repeatedly reread material. Students who were expected to teach the content to someone else after their revision period did better still.[3] What was found to be most interesting in other studies is that students using retrieval methods and testing for revision were also more resilient to the introduction of stress.[4]

Ebbinghaus' forgetting curve and spaced learning

Ebbinghaus' 140-year-old study examined the rate in which we forget things over time. The findings still hold power. However, the act of forgetting things and relearning them is what cements things into the brain.[5] Spacing out revision is more effective than cramming – we know that, but students should also know that the space between revisiting material should vary depending on how far away the examination is. A cyclical approach is required. An examination 12 months away necessitates revisiting covered material about once a month. A test in 30 days should have topics revisited every 3 days – intervals of roughly a tenth of the time available.[6]

Summary

Students: the more tests and past questions you do, in an environment as close to examination conditions as possible, the better you are likely to perform on the day. If you prefer to listen to music while you revise, tunes without lyrics will be far less detrimental to your memory and retention. Silence is most effective.[5] If you choose to study with friends, choose carefully – effort is contagious.[7]

1. Mayer, R. E., & Anderson, R. B. (1991). Animations need narrations: An experimental test of dual-coding hypothesis. *Journal of Education Psychology*, (83)4, 484-490.

2. Roediger III, H. L., & Karpicke, J.D. (2006). Test-enhanced learning: Taking memory tests improves long-term retention. *Psychological Science*, 17(3), 249-255.

3. Nestojko, J., Bui, D., Kornell, N. & Bjork, E. (2014). Expecting to teach enhances learning and organisation of knowledge in free recall of text passages. *Memory and Cognition*, 42(7), 1038-1048.

4. Smith, A. M., Floerke, V. A., & Thomas, A. K. (2016) Retrieval practice protects memory against acute stress. *Science*, 354(6315), 1046-1048.

5. Perham, N., & Currie, H. (2014). Does listening to preferred music improve comprehension performance? *Applied Cognitive Psychology*, 28(2), 279-284.

6. Cepeda, N. J., Vul, E., Rohrer, D., Wixted, J. T. & Pashler, H. (2008). Spacing effects in learning a temporal ridgeline of optimal retention. *Psychological Science*, 19(11), 1095-1102.

7. Busch, B. & Watson, E. (2019), *The Science of Learning*, 1st ed. Routledge.

CONTENTS

Computational thinking and programming skills - Paper 1

Section 1

☑

Specification

Section 2

☑

Computing concepts - Paper 2

Section 3

☑

Section 4

☑

MARK ALLOCATIONS

Green mark allocations[1] on answers to in-text questions through this guide help to indicate where marks are gained within the answers. A bracketed '1' e.g. [1] = one valid point worthy of a mark. There are often many more points to make than there are marks available so you have more opportunity to max out your answers than you may think.

TOPICS FOR PAPER 1
COMPUTATIONAL THINKING AND PROGRAMMING SKILLS

Information about Paper 1

Written exam: 2 hours
90 marks
50% of GCSE

Specification coverage

Computational thinking, code tracing, problem-solving, programming concepts including the design of effective algorithms and the designing, writing, testing and refining of code.

The content for this assessment will be drawn from subject content sections 3.1 and 3.2 of the specification.

Questions

A mix of multiple choice, short answer and longer answer questions assessing programming, practical problem-solving and computational thinking skills.

REPRESENTING ALGORITHMS

An **algorithm** is a sequence of steps that can be followed in order to complete a task. Examples include recipes, assembly instructions and directions.

An algorithm is not the same as a computer program. A computer program is one way of implementing an algorithm in a particular language, but it is the series of instructions and the order of those instructions that are the basis of any algorithm.

Computational thinking

Computational thinking is a process used to solve complex problems. It means formulating a problem and expressing its solution in such a way that a computer can carry it out.

There are two important stages involved:

- **Abstraction** involves identifying the key parts of the problem and removing any unnecessary detail so that it becomes easier to solve. For example, if a program is to be written to simulate a card game, the first task to be accomplished may be 'Shuffle the cards'. This is an abstraction – implementing it will involve specifying a way to randomise the order of 52 values representing the cards. We can refer to 'shuffle' throughout the program without specifying how it will be done.

- **Decomposition** means breaking down a complex problem into smaller, manageable parts which are easier to solve. This comprises the following steps:

  o Identify the main problem

  o List the main sub-problems, functions or tasks

  o Break these down into smaller sub-problems or sub-tasks which can then be completed separately. For example:

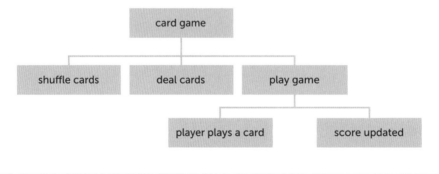

A self-driving car is being developed. The software has to be capable of distinguishing between an animal and a person crossing the road in front of the car.

(a) Define what is meant by **abstraction**. [2]

(b) Give **one** example of how abstraction could be used in developing this software. [1]

(a) Removing / hiding details of a problem[1] that are not relevant to a solution[1].

(b) Any example of something that can be removed or hidden, e.g. speed of the car[1], location at which something is crossing[1], whether it is on a pedestrian crossing[1], aerodynamic design of the vehicle[1].

USING FLOWCHARTS

Flowcharts are a useful tool that can be used to develop solutions to a problem. Standard flowchart symbols are shown below:

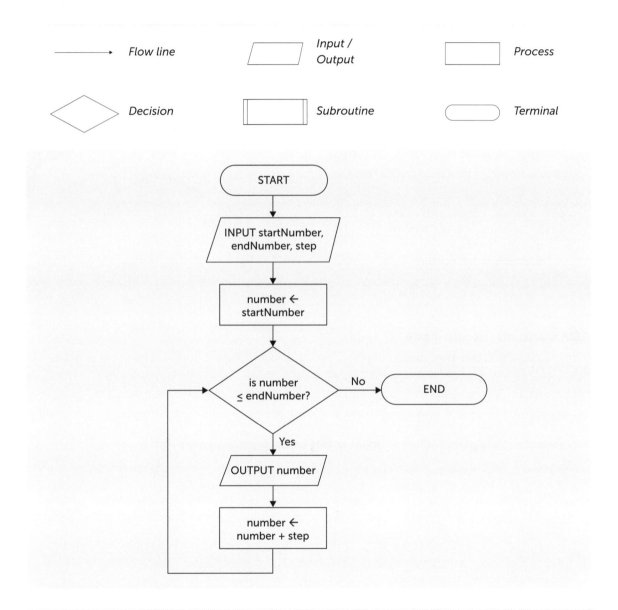

Look at the flowchart above.

(a) What will be output if the user enters 7, 50, 10 for the three input values? [2]

(b) What will be output if the user enters an end number which is less than the start number? [1]

(a) $7^{[1]}$, 17, 27, 37, $47^{[1]}$

(b) Nothing will be output.[1]

USING PSEUDO-CODE

The problem with using a flowchart to develop an algorithm is that it does not usually translate very easily into program code.

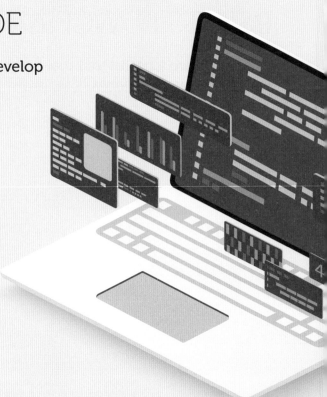

Pseudo-code is useful for developing an algorithm using programming-style constructs, but it is not an actual programming language. This means that a programmer can concentrate on figuring out how to solve the problem without worrying about the details of how to write each statement in the programming language that will be used.

Using pseudo-code, the algorithm shown in the flowchart on page 3 could be expressed like this:

```
input startNumber, endNumber, step
set number to startNumber
while number <= endNumber
    output(number)
    add step to number
endwhile
```

AQA standard pseudo-code

AQA has published a standard version of pseudo-code. This is defined in a file that can be downloaded from the AQA website. In an exam, where you are given pseudo-code, AQA will use the AQA standard version.

You do not have to use the AQA style of pseudo-code in your own work, when answering questions or describing algorithms. You will be awarded marks as long as your code is clear and consistent. **You should not use plain English or bullet points when describing algorithms.**

Some questions in the exam specify that you must use either a flowchart, pseudo-code or a high-level programming language you have studied to write or complete a program. Marks are awarded for correctly using syntax to represent programming constructs, whichever language you use. Answers for programming questions written in pseudo-code, natural English or bullets will not be awarded marks.

The algorithm shown above written in AQA standard pseudo-code would be written:

```
startNumber ← USERINPUT
endNumber ← USERINPUT
step ← USERINPUT
number ← startNumber
WHILE number ≤ endNumber
    OUTPUT number
    number ← number + step
ENDWHILE
```

Note that if there are three values to be input, when writing your own pseudo-code you should write three separate INPUT statements. Each INPUT statement is used to input a single value and assign it to a variable.

Assignment is shown using a backwards arrow ←.

INPUTS, PROCESSING AND OUTPUTS

Every problem to be solved using a computer involves input, processing and output.

- The **input** may be typed by someone at a keyboard, it may be a reading from a sensor such as a moisture, pressure or temperature sensor, or some other form of input.
- The data then has to be **processed** in some way – for example by sorting a list, performing calculations or using temperature readings to predict ice on the roads for example.
- **Output** is the end result after processing. This could be a printed report, a valve that is opened or closed, or graphics displayed on a screen.

DETERMINING THE PURPOSE OF AN ALGORITHM

You may be given a flowchart and asked to determine the purpose of the algorithm.

(a) Determine the purpose of this algorithm. [1]

(b) Write the algorithm using pseudo-code instead of a flowchart. [4]

(a) The purpose is to output the smallest of three numbers.[1]

(b) In pseudo-code:

a ← USERINPUT
b ← USERINPUT
c ← USERINPUT[1]
IF a < b THEN
    IF a < c THEN
        OUTPUT a
    ENDIF[1]
ELSE
    IF b < c THEN[1]
        OUTPUT b
    ELSE
        OUTPUT c
    ENDIF[1]
ENDIF[1]

Download the Python program solutions from **www.pgonline.co.uk**

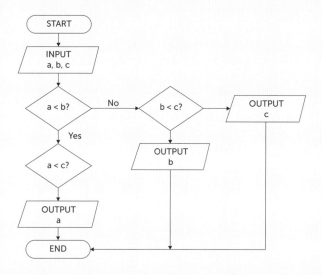

This algorithm uses a **nested selection** structure.

The IF statement has an IF statement nested inside it. In this example, the ELSE statement also has a nested IF statement.

TRACE TABLES

A **trace table** is used to show how the values of variables change during execution of a program.

As each line of code is executed, the current value of any variable or logical expression that is changed is written in the appropriate column of the table below. It is not necessary to fill in a cell if the value has not changed from the line above.

Example: Ben designs a flowchart for an algorithm to calculate the average number of hours students spend per week playing computer games. He uses test data for 3 students spending respectively 8, 10 and 12 hours playing games. This should result in an average of 10 hours.

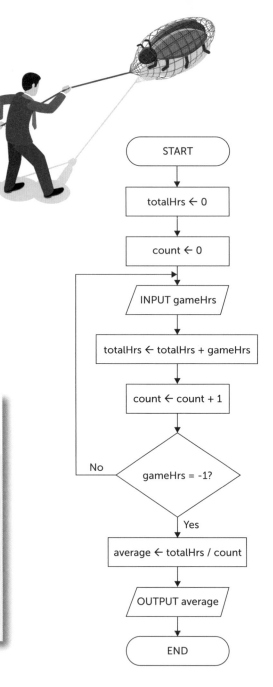

A trace table, shown below, has identified an error with the flowchart.

Describe how the algorithm could be corrected.   [3]

The input, gameHrs, should be tested right after it has been input.[1] However, a program cannot jump out of a loop before completing it.[1] Therefore, the input statement and the test for gameHrs = −1 should be placed at the end of the loop.[1] An initial input statement is required before entering the loop.[1]

Download the Python program solutions from **www.pgonline.co.uk**

gameHrs	totalHrs	count	gameHrs = −1?	average
	0	0		
8	8	1	No	
10	18	2	No	
12	30	3	No	
−1	29	4	Yes	7.25

Oops! The algorithm must be incorrect, since it produces the wrong answer.

EFFICIENCY OF ALGORITHMS

There are often many different ways of solving a problem. One algorithm may be much more efficient than another, performing the same task in a fraction of the time.

Example

Here is an algorithm that prints "Name is in the list" if a particular name is found in a list of 1,000 names. The names are held in an array or list named **aList**, and the first name is referred to as **aList[0]**.

```
nameSought ← USERINPUT
nameFound ← FALSE
FOR index ← 0 TO 999
    IF aList[index] = nameSought THEN
        nameFound ← TRUE
    ENDIF
ENDFOR
IF nameFound THEN
    OUTPUT "Name is in the list"
ELSE
    OUTPUT "Name not found"
ENDIF
```

Look at the pseudo-code provided above.

(a) Explain why this is such an inefficient algorithm.   [2]

(b) Complete lines 06, 09 and 11 in the more efficient algorithm given below.

```
01  nameSought ← USERINPUT
02  nameFound ← FALSE
03  index ← 0
04  WHILE NOT nameFound AND index < LEN(aList)
05      IF aList[index] = nameSought THEN
06          ............................
07          OUTPUT "Name is in the list"
08      ENDIF
09      ............................
10  ENDWHILE
11  IF ............... THEN
12      OUTPUT "Name not found"
13  ENDIF                                                                                 [3]
```

(a) *It is inefficient because even if the name is found right at the beginning of the list, the algorithm continues searching every item in the list.[1] It needs to terminate as soon as the item is found.[1]*

(b) *Line 06: nameFound ← TRUE[1]*
    Line 09: index ← index + 1[1]
    Line 11: IF NOT nameFound[1] or IF nameFound = FALSE[1]

SEARCHING ALGORITHMS

Binary search

A binary search can be used to search a list that is in numerical or alphabetical order. It works by repeatedly dividing in half the portion of the list that could contain the required data item.

Example: An ordered list of 12 numbers contains the following data items. To find whether the number 37 is in the list, start by examining the middle item in the list. This is the sixth item in this list of 12 numbers.

25	26	28	37	39	40	41	43	56	70	74	81

Stage 1: The middle item is 40. The search item 37 is less than 40. Discard all the items greater than or equal to 40.

25	26	28	37	39

Stage 2: The middle item is the third item, which is 28. 37 is greater than 28, so discard items less than or equal to 28.

37	39

Stage 3: The 'middle' item in a list of two numbers is the first one 37. This is the number we are searching for, so the algorithm can report that the number has been found. If we had been searching for, say, 36, we would know at this stage that the number is not in the list.

37

Sometimes the search item is found before completing all stages. If the search had been for the number 40, we would have found it at Stage 1, its position in the list would be returned and the algorithm could then be made to terminate.

Linear search

In a linear search, each item will be checked one by one in the list. This is very slow for large lists, but necessary if the list is not sorted. For large, sorted lists, a binary search is much more efficient as the number of items to be examined is halved at each stage.

A list of 14 names is shown below.

Anne	Bob	Chas	Eric	Fiona	Harry	Jo	Ken	Mona	Nahim	Geri	Peter	Steve	Zoe

(a) State which items are examined when looking for **Steve** using a binary search. [2]

(b) State which items are examined when looking for **Dave** using a binary search. [4]

(c) State how many items will be examined when looking for **Dave** in the list of names using a linear search. [1]

(a) Jo[1], Geri[1], (Steve will be the next search item).

(b) Jo[1], Chas[1], Fiona[1], Eric[1], (name not found).

(c) 14[1]

COMPARING AND CONTRASTING SEARCH ALGORITHMS

Binary search	Linear search
| ```
#Binary search
aList ← [2, 3, 11, 12, 15, 19, 23, 30, 36, 45]
OUTPUT("List to be searched:", aList)
found ← False
first ← 0
last ← LEN(aList) - 1
searchItem ← USERINPUT
WHILE NOT found AND first ≤ last
    midpt ← REAL_TO_INT((first+last) / 2)
    IF aList[midpt] = searchItem THEN
        found ← True
        index ← midpt
    ELSE
        IF aList[midpt] < searchItem THEN
            first ← midpt + 1
        ELSE
            last ← midpt - 1
        ENDIF
    ENDIF
ENDWHILE
IF found THEN
    OUTPUT("Found at position", index,
        "in the list")
ELSE
    OUTPUT("Item is not in the list")
ENDIF
``` | ```
#Linear search
aList ← [14, 2, 3, 11, 1, 9, 5, 8, 10, 6]
OUTPUT("List to be searched:", aList)
found ← False
index ← 0
searchItem ← USERINPUT
WHILE NOT found AND index < LEN(aList)
    IF aList[index] = searchItem THEN
        found ← True
    ELSE
        index ← index + 1
    ENDIF
ENDWHILE
IF found THEN
    OUTPUT(searchItem, "in position",
            index, "of the list")
ELSE
    OUTPUT("Item not found")
ENDIF
``` |

Linear search vs binary search

In a list of 1 million items, on average it will be necessary to examine 500,000 items to find a given item using a linear search. Using a binary search, only 20 items would need to be examined in a list of 1,000,000 items to find an item or to conclude that it is not in the list!

Give **two** reasons why you would use a linear search to find an item in a list. [2]

If the list is unsorted, it is not possible to do a binary search[1], so a linear sort must be performed.

On a very short list, the execution time for a linear search and a binary search is not significant[1] and a linear search is a simpler algorithm[1].

BUBBLE SORT

A bubble sort works by repeatedly going through the list to be sorted, swapping adjacent elements if they are in the wrong order.

To sort a list of n items, a maximum of n−1 passes is required. (The items may be alphabetical or numeric.)

Example

A list of 5 numbers 7, 3, 5, 9, 4 is to be sorted. Show the state of the list after each pass.

List	7	3	5	9	4	

Pass 1	3	7	5	9	4	
	3	5	7	9	4	
	3	5	7	9	4	
	3	5	7	4	9	Examine 5 items

After the first pass through the list, the largest number has 'bubbled' to the end of the list. In the second pass, we only need to compare the first four items.

Pass 2	3	5	7	4	9	
	3	5	7	4	9	
	3	5	4	7	9	Examine 4 items

Pass 3	3	5	4	7	9	
	3	4	5	7	9	Examine 3 items

Pass 4	3	4	5	7	9	Examine 2 items

The list is now sorted.

The list of animals **hamster, rabbit, dog, cat, goldfish**, is to be sorted in alphabetical order using a bubble sort. Show the state of the list after:

(a) Pass 1 [1]

(b) Pass 2 [1]

(a) hamster, dog, cat, goldfish, rabbit[1]

(b) dog, cat, goldfish, hamster, rabbit[1]

The bubble sort algorithm is not efficient for large lists. Note that in some cases, the algorithm may have sorted the list before performing the full number of passes. If no swaps are made during a particular pass, then the list must already be sorted. This condition could be tested and the algorithm could be made to terminate.

The algorithm for the bubble sort, including this modification, is given on page 12.

MERGE SORT

This is a very fast two-stage sort. In the first stage, the list is successively divided in half, forming two sublists, until each sublist is of length one.

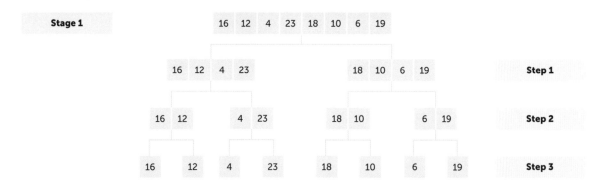

At the end of stage 1, all the elements have been separated out.

In the second stage, each pair of sublists is repeatedly merged to produce new sorted sublists until there is only one sublist remaining. This is the sorted list.

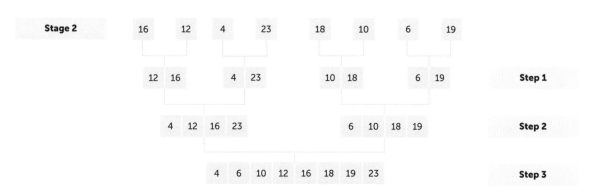

1. Write the list that results from merging the two lists 2, 5, 17, 38, 56 and 3, 4, 15, 19, 36   [1]

2. The following list is to be sorted using a merge sort algorithm.

Giraffe	Zebra	Monkey	Leopard	Hippo	Warthog	Rhino

(a) Describe the two stages of a merge sort algorithm.   [4]

(b) Write out the list after Step 2 of the Stage 2 process.   [2]

1. The list would be: 2, 3, 4, 5, 15, 17, 19, 36, 38, 56[1]

2. (a) Stage 1: The list is successively divided in half[1], forming two sublists[1], until each sublist is of length one[1].
   Stage 2: Each pair of sublists[1] is repeatedly merged[1] to produce new sorted sublists[1] until there is only one list remaining[1].

   (b) Giraffe, Leopard, Monkey, Zebra,[1]   Hippo, Rhino, Warthog[1]

COMPARING BUBBLE SORT AND MERGE SORT

Bubble sort vs Merge sort

The algorithm for the bubble sort is given below.

```
01  # Bubble sort
02  aList ← [17, 3, 7, 15, 13, 23, 20]
03  # get number of items in the array
04  numItems ← LEN(aList)
05  passNumber ← numItems - 1
06  swapMade ← True
07  WHILE passNumber > 0 AND swapMade
08      swapMade ← False
09      FOR j ← 0 TO passNumber - 1
10          IF aList[j] > aList[j + 1] THEN
11              temp ← aList[j]
12              aList[j] ← aList[j + 1]
13              aList[j + 1] ← temp
14              swapMade ← True
15          ENDIF
16      ENDFOR
17      passNumber ← passNumber - 1
18  ENDWHILE
19  OUTPUT("Sorted list: ", alist)
```

The Merge Sort algorithm is a more complex, **recursive** algorithm, meaning that it uses a subroutine that calls itself. (Recursion is beyond the scope of this course.)

The Bubble Sort algorithm, on the other hand, is an **iterative** algorithm, meaning that it uses WHILE and/or FOR loops, repeating the same steps many times.

For small datasets, the difference in execution time for each of these sorts will be insignificant. However, for very large data sets, the merge sort is many times faster. A bubble sort could take several hours to sort a dataset that a merge sort would sort in a few minutes or even seconds.

Look at the bubble sort algorithm above.

(a) State the line numbers of the Bubble Sort code given above which swaps two items in the list. [1]

(b) State the purpose of the variable named `temp`. [1]

(c) Explain the purpose of the variable named `swapMade`. [3]

(a) 11, 12, 13[1]

(b) temp is used to temporarily store the value of one of the variables to be swapped[1], so that when the second value overwrites it, the value can be moved from temp into the second variable[1].

(c) This is used to indicate when two values are swapped[1]. If swapMade is false, this shows that no values were swapped in a pass and the WHILE loop will then terminate[1] instead of doing more unnecessary passes[1]. This is a more efficient algorithm than one that always performs the full number of passes.

EXAMINATION PRACTICE

1. A pseudo-code algorithm is given below.

```
01   aList ← [3,6,7,9,13,15,16,19,20,24,26,29,36]
02   found ← False
03   n ← 0
04   x ← USERINPUT
05   WHILE NOT found AND n < LEN(aList)
06       OUTPUT (aList[n])
07       IF aList[n] = x THEN
08           found ← True
09       ELSE
10           n ← n + 1
11       ENDIF
12   ENDWHILE
13   IF found THEN
14       OUTPUT(x, n)
15   ELSE
16       OUTPUT("Invalid number")
17   ENDIF
```

(a) At line 05, what is the value of **LEN(aList)**? [1]

(b) The user enters 9 at line 04. What is printed at line 06 the first 3 times the while...endwhile loop is performed? [3]

(c) State what will be printed at line 14 if the user enters the number 9. [1]

(d) Explain the purpose of this algorithm. [2]

2. An array names holds **n** items. An algorithm for a bubble sort is given below.

```
01   swapMade ← True
02   WHILE swapMade
03       swapMade ← False
04       FOR index ← 0 TO n - 2
05           IF names[index] > names[index + 1] THEN
06               swap the names
07               swapMade ← True
08           ENDIF
09       ENDFOR
10       n ← n - 1
11   ENDWHILE
```

(a) Explain the purpose of the variable **swapMade** in the algorithm. [2]

(b) Write the code for "swap the names" in line 06. [3]

(c) The list **names** contains the following:

| Edna | Adam | Victor | Charlie | Jack | Ken | Maria |

Write the contents of the list after each of the first two times the WHILE loop is executed. [2]

(d) Explain how many times the WHILE loop will be executed before the program terminates. [2]

3. For each of the following activities, state whether they are examples of abstraction, decomposition or algorithm design.
   (a) Planning a series of step-by-step instructions specifying how a computer will solve a problem. [1]
   (b) Identifying the sub-problems involved in solving a problem, and further breaking down the sub-problems into ones which can be solved more easily. [1]
   (c) Removing unnecessary details of a problem that are not relevant to a solution. [1]

4. (a) An algorithm is given below.

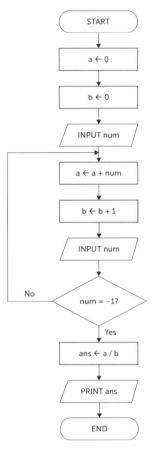

Complete the trace table to show how the variables change, and what will be output, if the numbers 3, 8, 2, 5, −1 are entered. [4]

num	a	b	ans
	0	0	0
3	3	1	0
8			

(b) State the purpose of the algorithm. [1]

VARIABLES, CONSTANTS, ASSIGNMENTS

Data used in a program is stored in memory locations while the program is running. A **variable** is a memory location holding a data item which may change value during program execution.

The table below shows the different data types found in programming languages such as Python or VB.

Data type	Type of data	Examples
Integer	A whole number	3, −170, 176500
Real/float	A number with a decimal point	3.142, 78.0, −0.5678
Character/char	A single character or symbol that can be typed	A, #, @, 6, !
String	Zero or more characters enclosed in quote marks	"yes", "Hi John"
Boolean	Can only take the value True or False	True, False

Some programming languages (but not Python) allow the use of **constants**. The value of a constant cannot change during the execution of the program.

```
const VAT = 0.2
```

A **variable name** can be a mixture of letters and numbers, but should start with a letter. Uppercase letters and lowercase letters may be used – note, for example, that the variable name `Total` is treated as different from `total`. The **value** of a variable (not its name) can change during program execution.

CamelCase is commonly used to separate words making up a variable name; for example, `totalCost`, `studentName`. Variable names by convention start with a lowercase letter, and constants are usually written in uppercase and 'snakecase' such as MAX_NUMBER_OF_PLAYERS.

Using a naming convention such as this helps to reduce errors in writing variable names in a program. If no convention has been used, it can be difficult to remember whether, for example, a total cost is named `totalCost`, `totalcost`, `Totalcost`, `total_cost` or something else. It also aids other programmers who may need to update a pre-existing program.

A **variable** is **assigned** a value in Python using the = sign.

```
costPrice = 15.65
count = count + 3          (This increases the value of the variable  count  by 3)
under12 = True
studentName = "Higgins, P"    (Python also allows the use of a single quote)
```

A game is being programmed.

(a) (i) Choose a meaningful variable name for the highest score in the game. [1]

   (ii) Set the highest score to 25. [1]

(b) (i) Choose a meaningful variable name for the name of a player. [1]

   (ii) Set the player's name to "Santos". [1]

(c) Explain the reason why variable names are commonly written using 'camelCase'. [2]

(a) e.g. (i) highScore[1] (ii) highScore = 25[1] (b) (i) playerName[1] (ii) playerName = "Santos"[1]

(c) So they are consistent[1], easier to remember[1] and therefore reduce programming errors.[1]

INPUT / OUTPUT

Python will generally be used in programming code throughout this section. However, you need to be able to recognise AQA pseudo-code statements, which may appear in exam questions.

When data needs to be input, the user is typically prompted to type something, and whatever they type is assigned to a variable. The Python input statement shown below does this in a single line:

```
name = input("Please enter your name: ")
```

In AQA pseudo-code, this would be written without the user prompt:

```
OUTPUT "Please enter your name: "
name ← USERINPUT
```

STRING CONVERSION OPERATIONS

Built-in functions are used to convert numbers into strings and vice versa.

Function		Description	Example	Returns
Python	Pseudo-code			
float(x)	STRING_TO_REAL(StringExp)	converts a string to a real (floating point) number	float("7.45")	7.45
int(x)	STRING_TO_INT(StringExp)	converts string to integer	int("3562)	356
str(x)	REAL_TO_STR(Real_Exp)	converts a real number to a string value	str(67.0)	"67.0"
str(x)	INT_TO_STR(IntExp)	converts integer to string	str(67)	"67"

Input

In Python, all input is accepted as a **string** data type. Therefore, if a number is being input, it must be converted to either an **integer** or **real** (**floating point**) number, whichever is appropriate.

```
visitors = int(input("Enter number of visitors: "))
roomLength = float(input("Enter room length in metres: "))
```

The print statement is used to output data to the screen. Example: Write Python code which asks the user to enter two integer numbers representing the length and breadth of a rectangle, then calculates and prints the area.

```
length = int(input("Enter length: "))
breadth = int(input("Enter breadth: "))
print("Area = ", length * breadth)
```

You can use the concatenation operator '+' instead of a comma ',' in a print statement, but you cannot mix strings and numbers. Numbers must first be converted to strings e.g:

```
print("Area = " + str(area))
```

Write an input statement that asks the user to enter a telephone number. [2]

```
phoneNumber =[1] input("Enter your telephone number: ")[1]
```

PROGRAMMING CONCEPTS

Arithmetic operators		
Pseudo-code	**Python**	**Meaning**
+	+	Addition
−	−	Subtraction
*	*	Multiplication
/	/	Division
MOD	%	Modulus
DIV	//	Quotient
^	**	Exponentiation

Relational operators		
Pseudo-code	**Python**	**Meaning**
=	==	Equal to
≠	!=	Not equal to
<	<	Less than
≤	<=	Less than or equal to
>	>	Greater than
≥	>=	Greater than or equal to

MOD returns the remainder when one integer is divided by another. For example,

x ← 22 MOD 5 will assign the value 2 to x   (In Python, x = 22 % 5)

x ← 15 MOD 5 will assign the value 0 to x   (In Python, x = 15 % 5)

DIV gives the quotient, so x ← 17 DIV 5 assigns 3 to x, and 22 DIV 5 assigns 4 to x.

(In Python, x = 17 // 5 and x = 22 // 5)

Sequence, selection and iteration

There are three basic control structures in all high-level imperative languages such as Python, C# or VB.NET. These are **sequence**, **selection** and **iteration**.

Sequence is simply two or more statements written and executed one after the other in sequence.

A **selection** statement comprises an **IF** statement and a **relational operator** forming part of a **Boolean expression**. Variables of the **Boolean data type** can only be True or False. The Boolean operations **AND, OR** and **NOT** are used to combine two or more conditions.

Tip: A selection statement such as

```
if flag = True:
```

can alternatively be written as

```
if flag:
```

What will these Boolean conditions, written in Python, evaluate to?

(a) `"Fred" != "fred"`   [1]

(b) `1 <= 4 and 7 <= 7`   [1]

(c) What will be output by the following statements?

```
a = 5
b = 2 * a
c = a + b
if (a = b) OR (b <= c):
    print("True")
else
    print("False")
```
[1]

(d) Write the condition statement
```
    if listSorted = False:
```
in a shorter form.   [1]

(a) *True*[1]

(b) *True*[1]

(c) *True*[1]

(d) `if not listSorted:`[1]

SELECTION

Selection statements include **if ...**, **if ... else** and **if ... elif ... else** statements.

An algorithm to check a user password has been written in pseudo-code.
This has been rewritten on the right using Python:

```
password ← USERINPUT
IF password ≠ "SP123" THEN
    OUTPUT "Invalid password"
ENDIF
```

```
password = input("Please enter
                    password: ")
if password != "SP123":
    print("Invalid password")
```

1. Write Python statements to ask a user to input his or her age, and output "You are old enough to drive" or "You are not old enough to drive" depending on whether the age input is 17 or over. [3]

```
age = int(input("Please enter your age: " ))[1]
if age >= 17:[1]
    print("You are old enough to drive")
else:
    print("You are not old enough to drive")[1]
```

Nested selection statements

An **IF** statement may be nested inside another **IF** statement. For example, suppose we wanted to output the largest of the three numbers entered. The Python code could be written:

```
if num1 >= num2 and num1 >= num3:
    print("maximum is ", num1)
else:
    if num2 >= num1 and num2 >= num3:
        print("maximum is ", num2)
    else:
        print("maximum is ", num3)
```

The elif clause in Python (ELSE IF in AQA pseudo-code) is a useful selection tool when there are several alternative paths depending on the value of a variable:

```
if member = "Junior":
    print("entry = 2.0")
elif member = "Senior":
    print("entry = 3.0")
elif member = "Special":
    print("entry = 0.0")
else:
    print("Member type must be Junior, Senior or Special.")
```

2. Write a Boolean condition to test whether `result` is between 1 and 10. [1]

```
if result >= 1 and result <= 10:[1]
```

(*Tip:* Writing `if result >= 1 and <= 10:` is incorrect and will score no marks.)

ITERATION

A **FOR … ENDFOR** loop is a **definite count controlled** loop. A count is automatically incremented each time the loop is performed.

The code below will print all the numbers from 1 to 10.

In pseudo-code:	**In Python:**
```FOR count ← 1 TO 10 OUTPUT count ENDFOR```	```for count in range(1,11): print(count)```

1. Complete the following Python program, which allows the user to enter a start number and an end number, and prints out all the numbers in between which are divisible by either 3 or 7, or both.

```
startNum = int(input("Enter start number: "))
endNum = int(input("Enter end number: "))
for count ........................
    if count % 3 == 0 .......................
        ........................
```
[3]

```
startNum = int(input("Enter start number: "))
endNum = int(input("Enter end number: "))
for count in range(startNum, endNum + 1)[1]
    if (count % 3 == 0) or (count % 7 == 0):[1]
        print(count)[1]
```

Nested iteration

You can have one loop nested inside another.

Example: Display all the multiplication tables between 2 and 10.

```
for table in range(2, 11):
    for n in range(1,11):
        answer = table * n
        print(table, " x ", n, " = ", answer)
```

2. There are two loops in the above code.
   (a) State whether they count-controlled or condition-controlled loops. [1]
   (b) How many times will the print statement be executed? Explain your answer. [2]

   (a) A FOR loop is a count-controlled loop[1].

   (b) The print statement is executed 90 times.[1] The outer FOR loop is executed 9 times.[1] Each time the outer FOR loop is executed, the inner loop is executed 10 times.[1]

CONDITION CONTROLLED ITERATION

WHILE...ENDWHILE, **REPEAT...UNTIL** and **DO...WHILE** are examples of **indefinite**, or **condition controlled**, iteration.

WHILE...ENDWHILE loop

A WHILE ... ENDWHILE loop is controlled by a Boolean condition which is checked **before** the loop is entered. In the Python program below, if `mark = -1` before entering the while loop, none of the statements in the loop will be executed. `numMarks` will be 0 and the program will crash with an **execution error** when it reaches the last line.

```
total = 0
numMarks = 0
mark = int(input("Enter next mark: "))
while mark != -1:
    total = total + mark
    numMarks = numMarks + 1
    mark = int(input("Enter next mark: "))
#endwhile
print("Average mark =", total/numMarks)
```

1. Explain what will happen when the following pseudo-code is coded and executed:

```
total ← 0
x ← 0
WHILE x ≠ 100
    total ← total + x
    x ← x + 3
ENDWHILE
OUTPUT("total = ", x) [2]
```

x will never be 100[1], so the program will result in an infinite loop[1]. x = 0, 3, 6,... 99, 102[1]

REPEAT...UNTIL and DO...WHILE loops

REPEAT...UNTIL and DO...WHILE loops are controlled by a Boolean condition which is checked at the *end* of the loop. They are therefore always performed at least once.

Note: Python does not have a REPEAT...UNTIL or a DO...WHILE construct.

```
number ← 1
REPEAT
    number ← number * 2
    OUTPUT number
UNTIL number > 1000
```

```
number ← 1
DO
    number ← number * 2
    OUTPUT number
WHILE number ≤ 1000
```

2. (a) Which of the following gives the number of times the above REPEAT loop is performed?

    A. 9   B. 10   C. 500   [1]

(b) Rewrite the algorithm using a Python WHILE loop.   [2]

   (a) 10[1]

   (b) number = 1
     while number <= 1000:[1]
       *number = number * 2[1]*
       print(number)

DATA STRUCTURES

An **array** is a data structure used to hold several items of the same type.

For example, an array could contain the names of the days of the week. Python uses **lists** rather then arrays, but in many ways, they operate in a similar fashion.

In Python, a list is initialised like this:

```
day = ["Sun", "Mon", "Tues", "Wed", "Thurs", "Fri", "Sat"]
```

Items are referred to using their **index**, or position in the list, starting at 0. Thus the third item (Tues) in this list is referred to as **day[2]**.

A list filled with 100 zeros may be initialised with the statement: **day = [0] * 100**

Example: Write a program to enter the number of customers visiting a shop each day of the week and then print out the total number of customers for the week.

```
01  day = ["Sun", "Mon", "Tues", "Wed", "Thurs", "Fri", "Sat"]
02  customers = [0]*7   # or, customers = [0,0,0,0,0,0,0]
03  totalCustomers = 0
04  for n in range(7):
05      print(day[n] + ": ")
06      customers[n] = int(input("Enter number of customers: "))
07      totalCustomers = totalCustomers + customers[n]
08  for n in range(7):
09      print(day[n],customers[n])
10  print("Total customers",totalCustomers)
```

1. What will be output at line 05 the third time the FOR loop is executed? [1]
2. Define an array called numbers holding five numbers 37, 76, 55, 91, 23.

   Write code to reverse the order of the numbers, storing them in a second array called **reverseNumbers**. Print out the contents of **reverseNumbers**. [5]

```
1. Tues:  [1]
2. numbers = [37, 76, 55, 91, 23] [1]
   reverseNumbers = [0,0,0,0,0] [1]    #or, reverseNumbers = [0] * 5
   for index in range(5): [1]
       reverseNumbers[index] = numbers[4-index] [1]
   print("Reverse numbers: ", reverseNumbers) [1]
```

Records

The RECORD data structure is not used in Python. Records are covered in **Section 7, Relational databases and SQL**.

An example of a record definition is:

```
RECORD student
    StudentID  : string
    Surname    : string
    firstname  : string
    YearOfBirth : integer
ENDRECORD
```

TWO-DIMENSIONAL ARRAYS / LISTS

An array may have two or more dimensions. A two-dimensional array or list named sales could hold the number of properties sold each quarter (Jan–March, April–June, July–September, October–December) by three different branches of an estate agent. An index number is used to reference an array value.

Index	0	1	2	3
0	56	87	92	43
1	167	206	387	54
2	22	61	52	14

Three branches (rows labelled 0, 1, 2)

The index for both row and column of the array/list starts at 0. In Python the list may be defined as:

```
sales = [[56,87,92,43],[167,206,387,54],[22,61,52,14]]
```

The number of properties sold in Quarter 4 by Branch 1 is held in **sales[0][3]** and has the value 43.

1. The three branches of the estate agency are known as Branch A, Branch B and Branch C.
   (a) Write code to output the sales figure for Branch C for the period April–June. [1]
   (b) What will be output? [1]
2. Write a program to ask a user to enter the name and five race times in seconds for each of 3 competitors, and display the average time for each competitor. [8]

```
1. (a) print(sales[2][1]) [1]   (b) 61 [1]
2. name = ["","",""] [1]
   totalTime = [0,0,0] [1]
   averageTime = [0,0,0] [1]
   raceTime = [ [0,0,0,0,0],
                [0,0,0,0,0],
                [0,0,0,0,0] ] [1]
   for c in range(3): [1]
      name[c] = input("Enter competitor name: ") [1]
      for race in range(5): [1]
          raceTime[c][race] = int(input("Enter race time: ")) [1]
          totalTime[c] = totalTime[c] + raceTime[c][race] [1]
      averageTime[c] = totalTime[c] / 5 [1]
      print("Average race Time for ",name[c], averageTime[c]) [1]
```

STRING MANIPULATION

Concatenating and indexing strings

Concatenating means 'joining together'. So:

```
"Alan" + "Bates"  evaluates to  "AlanBates"
"2" + "3"  evaluates to  "23"
```

Each character in a string can be referenced by its **index**, starting at 0.

Thus, if `studentName = "Jumal"`

then `studentName[0]` will contain `"J"` and `studentName[3]` will contain `"a"`.

Substrings

Using indexing, you can isolate a single character or several characters in a string. For example, if the first three characters of a 9-character product code represent product type, and the next four characters represent the year of manufacture, you can isolate these strings using different **string methods** and string handling operations in Python:

```
productCode = "GAR201834"
productType = productCode[0:3]
year = productCode[3:7]
print("ProductType = ", productType)
print("Year = ", year)
```

This will print:

```
Product type = GAR
Year = 2018
```

Write a program which asks the user to enter a firstname and a surname, and outputs the surname followed by a space and the initial letter of the firstname. [4]

```
firstname = input("Enter firstname: ")[1]
surname = input("Enter surname: ")[1]
initial = firstname[0][1]
print(surname + " " + initial)[1]
```

String functions and methods

Example: **myString** is defined with the following assignment statement:

```
myString = "My name is Kenneth Lee"
```

To find the length of this string: `aLength = len(myString)`
This will assign 22 to **aLength**.

To find the starting index of the name "Kenneth":   `pos = myString.find("Kenneth")`
This assigns 11 to **pos**. If the substring is not found, **pos** will evaluate to −1.

To find the first **n** characters of a string: `nChars = myString[0:n]`

To convert a character to its ASCII value: `aVal = ord("A")`
This will return 65 in **aVal**. This would be written in AQA pseudocode as: `CHAR_TO_CODE('A')`

To convert an ASCII character code to a character: `myChar = chr(106)`
This will return "**b**" in **myChar**. This would be written in AQA pseudocode as: `CODE_TO_CHAR(106)`

SUBROUTINES

A **subroutine** is a named block of code, separate from the main program, which can be executed (called) simply by writing its name in a program statement.

There are two types of subroutine, **functions** and **procedures**, which are usually defined and called slightly differently.

A **function** returns a value to a variable specified in the call statement. Python has many built-in functions, some of which you have already used. `input`, `int` and `len` are examples of functions you have used. Notice how these functions are called:

`myName = input("Enter name")` assigns the user input to variable `myName`

`"Enter name"` is the **parameter** (or **argument**) passed to the function.

`num = int("345")` assigns the integer `345` to variable `num`.

`sLength = len("This is a string")` will return `16` in `sLength`.

---

1. Name the parameters passed to the functions `int` and `len` in the above statements. [2]

   `"345"`[1], `"This is a string"`[1]

A **procedure** does not return a value. It is called by simply writing its name, with parameters in brackets. You have used the built-in procedure `print`, for example: `print("Answer is", x)`

Procedures and functions are both written in the same way in Python. The only difference is that a function contains a **return** statement, and a procedure does not.

All Python subroutines start with a statement beginning with the word **def** and ending with a colon. All subsequent statements are indented.

This function converts a Celsius temperature to Fahrenheit:

```
def convertToF(cTemp):
    fTemp = (cTemp * 9/5) + 32
    return fTemp
```

To call the function and assign the Fahrenheit temperature to `tempInF`:

```
celsiusTemp = input("Enter temperature in celsius")
tempInF = convertToF(celsiusTemp)
```

`celsiusTemp` is the **parameter** (or **argument**) passed to the function. Within the function, the parameter is referred to as `cTemp`. Note: AQA uses only the term *parameter*, not *argument*.

---

2. Write a statement to call the procedure `greeting(aName)`, passing it the parameter `"Helen"`. What will be output? [2]

   ```
   def greeting(aName):
       print("Hello " + aName)
   ```
   To call the procedure: `greeting("Helen")`[1]   Output: Hello Helen[1]

THE STRUCTURED APPROACH

Decomposition of a problem involves breaking down a problem into subroutines or **modules**. This helps to produce **structured code**.

The structured approach includes **modularised programming** using **parameters and local variables**. **Clear**, **well-documented code** should include **comments** to explain what the code is intended to do.

Using subroutines in programs has many advantages

- Makes debugging and maintaining the program easier as subroutines are usually no more than a page of code and are separate from the main program
- Subroutines can be tested separately and shown to be correct
- A particular subroutine can be called several times in the same program, and may also be saved in a subroutine library to be used in other programs

Python has a library of useful modules which can be imported into a program.

A subroutine may declare its own **local variables**, which exist only while the subroutine is executing. They are only accessible within the subroutine. This is important because if the value of a variable having an identical name in the main program is changed, this will not affect the local variable in the subroutine.

Generating a random number

The `randint()` function generates a random number. To use it, you must first import the Python library module **random** by writing the statement `import random` at the start of the program. Then, to generate a random number num between a range of integers a and b:

```
num = random.randint(a,b)
```

Random numbers are often used in modelling. For example, suppose an ice cream van is visited by between 100 and 500 people each day during a given period. The owner wants to model the total number of customers, assuming a random number of customers in that range each day.

```
import random                    #import a library module
def totalFootfall(minCust, maxCust, days):
    totalCustomers = 0
    for day in range(days): #day is a local variable
        dailyCustomers = random.randint(minCust, maxCust)
        print(dailyCustomers)
        totalCustomers = totalCustomers + dailyCustomers
    return totalCustomers

customers = ................................
print("Total customers for period: ",customers)
```

Look at the code above. Complete the statement to call the function `totalFootfall()` for a 30-day period. [2]

```
customers = totalFootfall(100,500,30[1])[1]
```

ICE

ICE CREAM

ROBUST AND SECURE PROGRAMMING

Data validation techniques are used to check the validity of data entered by the user.

Data validation

You should be able to write simple routines to validate input data. The following validation checks are examples of simple data validation:

- **Length check:** a string entered by a user must be greater than or equal to a minimum length.

- **Presence check:** a string should not be empty.

- **Range check:** data must lie within a given range.

---

1. A user is required to enter a 6-character ID in order to register on a website.
   Complete line 02 in the code below to ensure that a valid ID has been entered. [2]

```
01  userID = input("Please enter a 6-character ID: ")
02  while ..............................
03      userID = input("ID must be 6 characters: please re-enter: ")
04  print("UserID accepted")
```

while len(userID)[1] != 6:[1]

Authentication routines

Authentication is a process used to test that a person is who they claim to be. Methods of authentication include a simple user ID and password, a PIN number or more complex biometric methods such as fingerprint or facial recognition. This helps to prevent unauthorised access.

Below is a simple authentication routine which checks that a password entered by the user is the same as the one held on file. (Assume this has been read into a variable named **validPassword**.)

```
password = input("Please enter password: ")
if password == validPassword:
    print("Password accepted")
else
    print("Invalid - Passwords don't match")
```

---

2. A date of birth field has been validated.

   (a) Explain how the validated date of birth field may still be incorrect. [2]

   (b) Give **one** example of an invalid date of birth that should not be accepted. [1]

   (a) A user may enter a date of birth of 10/05/2005[1], but their actual birthday was 19/05/2005.[1] This would be accepted by the computer as a valid date of birth.

   (b) Any year or date in the future[1], any day greater than 31 or less than 1[1], any month greater than 12 or less than 1[1]. E.g. 32/01/2005 or 31/02/2005.

TESTING

The **purpose of testing** is to ensure that for any input, the program always works correctly. Your program may give correct results for some inputs, but does it work correctly for all possible inputs, including invalid ones?

Syntax and logic errors

A **syntax error** will prevent your program from running. It is typically caused by a mistake in the spelling or 'grammar' of your code. For example `primt("Hello World")`. Syntax errors will be detected and reported by the compiler or interpreter.

A **logic error** is harder to spot. Your program will run but may crash or give an incorrect or unexpected output. Common examples involve the use of greater than or less than symbols, for example: using `x > 5` instead of `x >= 5` which could affect loop conditions or range checks. Another example of a common logic error is missing brackets in mathematics calculations, e.g.:

```
VAT = (orderTotal - discount) * taxRate  gives a different answer to:
VAT = orderTotal - discount * taxRate
```

Using a well thought-out test plan, with the expected results manually calculated first, should reveal any logic errors. Using a trace table may help to find and correct the errors.

Selecting and using suitable test data

Test data should include:

- **normal (typical) data**, using examples of typical data that the program is designed to handle.
- **boundary (extreme) data** which includes both ends of the allowed range (e.g. 1–50) as well as invalid data that should not be allowed, just outside this range. For example, if a range of 0 to 50 needs to be tested, then the boundary data would be -1, 0, 50 ,51.
- **erroneous data** - data of the wrong type, for example non-numeric characters in a numeric field.

A test plan which includes the expected results for each test should be drawn up even before the program is coded.

Example: John has written a program to input and validate daily temperatures recorded in a particular month. The temperature is never above 35 or below 0.

No.	Test purpose	Test data	Expected outcome	Actual outcome
1	Check valid boundary data	0, 35	Input is accepted	
2	Check invalid boundary data	−1, 36	Error message displayed and user asked to enter number again	
3	Check valid typical entry	12	Input is accepted	
4	Check erroneous entry	xx, 2+6	Error message displayed and user asked to enter number again	

EXAMINATION PRACTICE

1. An organisation stores data about its employees. State the most suitable data type for storing the following data:

    (a) employee surname [1]

    (b) whether or not the employee has signed a contract of employment [1]

    (c) the number of days holiday they are entitled to per annum [1]

    (d) an employee's monthly salary [1]

2. Henry has written a Python program. It is intended to accept as input the height of visitors queuing at a turnstile for a fairground ride. A message "Too small for this ride!" is printed and the turnstile remains closed for children under 1.2m tall.

    The line numbers are not part of the program. They are for reference only.

    ```
    01  print("Input height of visitor: ")
    02  input(height)
    03  if height <= 1.2:
    04     print("Too small for this ride!")
    ```

    The program contains a syntax error.

    (a) State the line number where the syntax error occurs. [1]

    (b) Rewrite the statement using correct syntax. [2]

    The program contains a logic error.

    (c) State the line number where the logic error occurs. [1]

    (d) Correct the statement so that the program works correctly. [1]

3. State what will be output by the following Python code snippets:

    (a)
    ```
    x = (5 + 4) * 3
    y = 5 + (4 * 3)
    if x >= y:
        z = True
    else:
        z = False
    print(z)
    ```
    [1]

    (b) `print((12 + 4) % 3)` [1]

    (c) `print((12 + 4) // 3)` [1]

4. The Boolean condition `"a" in myName` returns TRUE if the string `myName` contains the character "a".

    (a) Write a Boolean condition that evaluates to TRUE if the integer `count` does NOT contain the digit 7. [3]

    (b) Write a program to print all the numbers between 1 and 100 except those that contain the digit 7 or those that are divisible by 5. E.g. 1, 2, 3, 4, 6, 8, 9, 11, 12... [3]

5. Write a Python program which accepts a mark entered by the user, and prints it together with the word "Fail" if the mark is below 50, "Pass" if the mark is between 50 and 64, "Merit" if the mark is between 65 and 79, and "Distinction" if the mark is 80 or more. [6]

6. An array **names** holds the names of 6 children called Anna, Dan, Peter, Sara, Vera, Zoe.

   (a) Complete the program code below to print the names of the 6 children on separate lines.

   ```
   name = ["Anna","Dan","Peter","Sara","Vera","Zoe"]
   for .....................
   ...........................
   ```
   [2]

   (b) What type of search would you use to find out whether a particular name was in the array? Justify your answer. [2]

7. A hockey team played 6 matches last year against each of five teams A, B, C, D and E.

   The number of wins, losses, and draws achieved in matches played against each team is recorded in a 2-dimensional list named **results** shown below.

   (a) The wins against team B are held in results[1][0].

   State which element of the list holds the losses against Team D. [1]

   (b) Complete the Python code below to calculate and print the total number of wins, draws and losses scored overall. [5]

	Wins	Draws	Losses
A	3	1	2
B	4	0	2
C	3	3	0
D	2	0	4
E	5	0	1

   ```
   results = [[3,1,2], [4,0,2], [3,3,0], [2,0,4], [5,0,1]]
   wins = 0
   draws = 0
   losses = 0
   for ...........................
       wins = wins + results[row][0]
       draws = ....................
       losses = ....................
   print(........................)
   ```

8. A username is created by concatenating the first two letters of their first name, the first three letters of their surname and a date of birth recorded as a string in the format ddmmyy.

   For example, COLIN BRADY, born 17/01/08 would have username COBRA170108.

   (a) What would be the username assigned to MABEL GREEN, born 29/02/2012? [1]

   (b) Complete the program code snippet below to assign a username to JAYDEN BULLINGDEN, born 12/05/2009. [4]

   ```
   firstname = "JAYDEN"
   surname = .....................
   dob = .........................
   username = firstname[0:2] + ................................
   ```

9. The Python program below has been written to simulate throwing two dice a number of times. It should then print the number of times the two dice throws were equal, and the number of times both throws were a 6.

The line numbers are not part of the program. They are used for reference purposes only.

```
01   import random
02   e = 0
03   double6 = 0
04   throws = int(input("Throw each die how many times? "))
05   for n in range(throws):
06       throw1 = random.randint(1,6)
07       throw2 = random.randint(1,6)
08       total = throw1 + throw2
09       if throw1 == throw2:
10           e = e + 1
11       if total == 12:
12           double6 = double6 + 1
13           print("Double 6!")
14   print(e, double6)
```

(a) Give the line number where selection is first used in the program. [1]

(b) Give the line number where iteration is first used in the program. [1]

(c) Explain what happens in line 04. [3]

(d) Explain what happens in line 06. [2]

(e) Suggest a more meaningful identifier for e, initialised in line 02. [1]

(f) The two dice are each thrown 9 times, with the results:

1 4,   4 3,   5 2,   5 5,   2 4,   6 6,   3 4,   5 1,   2 2.

What will be output at line 14? [2]

10. A customer registering with an online store for the first time is required to input data including their email, a password, their date of birth and postcode.

Describe **three** validation checks that could be carried out on this data. [6]

11. The procedure below, shown in lines 01 to 04, displays the times table from 2 to 10 for **aNum**. For example, if the user inputs 6, the procedure will print:

6 x 2 = 12
6 x 3 = 18 etc

```
01   def timesTable(aNum):
02       for n in range(2,11):
03           xTimesN = aNum * n
04           print(str(aNum) + " x " + str(n) + " = " + str(xTimesN))
05   tableToPrint = .........................................
06   ............................
```

(a) Complete the statements at lines 05 and 06 to print a table of the user's choice. [4]

(b) Name a local variable in the procedure. [1]

(c) Name a function used within the procedure, and describe what it does. [2]

12. The function **triangle()** has 3 parameters a, b, c and returns True if $a^2 = b^2 + c^2$

(a) Write Python code to complete lines 02 and 03 of this function.   [2]

```
01  def triangle(a,b,c):
02      x = ...................
03      y = ..................
04      if x == y:
05          return True
06      else:
07          return False
```

(b) Write statements to pass three integers sideA, sideB, sideC to the function and print "Right-angled" if the function returns True, or "Not right-angled" if it returns False.   [3]

13. The following partially completed program validates a user password. The user is permitted three attempts to enter the password correctly before being locked out.

```
01  savedPassword = "Black&Bird34"
02  validPassword = False
03  attempts = 0
04  while not validPassword and .....................:
05      userPassword = input("Enter password: ")
06      if userPassword == savedPassword:
07          ........................
08          attempts = 3
09      else:
10          attempts = attempts + 1
11          print("Invalid password")
12  if validPassword:
13      print("Please continue")
14  else:
15      print("Locked out")
```

(a) Here is a list of data types.

integer   float   character   string   Boolean

Complete the table below to show the data types of the variables given in the table.   [3]

Variable	Variable type
savedPassword	
validPassword	
attempts	

(b) Complete line 04 of the program.   [1]

(c) Complete line 07 of the program.   [1]

(d) Write alternative code for line 12 which will perform the same function.   [1]

(e) Explain why a user is allowed no more than three attempts to enter the correct password.   [3]

14. An airline booking service permits up to four bags per passenger. A segment of Python code has been written to validate this input.

```
01  int(input("Enter number of bags", bagCount))
02  if bagCount >= 0 or bagCount <= 4:
03      print("Bag allowance OK")
04  else:
05      print("Invalid bag allowance")
```

(a) The code contains a logic error at line 02.

    (i) State what is meant by a logic error. [1]

    (ii) Give an amended version of line 02 that corrects the error. [1]

(b) Identify **one** syntax error in the code. [1]

(c) Complete the test plan below to check that the valid range for bags is correct. [5]

No.	Test purpose	Test data	Expected outcome	Actual outcome
1	Check lowest valid boundary number		Input is accepted	
2	Check highest valid boundary number		Input is accepted	
3	Check invalid boundary data		Error message, user asked to re-enter number	
4	Check valid entry		Input is accepted	
5	Check erroneous entry		Error message, user asked to re-enter number	

15. Algorithm 1 (lines 04–06) and Algorithm 2 (line 09) shown in the Python code below both perform the same calculation and print the same answer. Explain why the second algorithm is more efficient than the first one. [3]

```
01  start = int(input("Enter start number: "))
02  end = int(input("Enter end number: "))
03  # Algorithm 1
04  sum = 0
05  for n in range(start, end + 1):
06      sum = sum + n
07  print("Algorithm 1: sum = ",sum)
08  # Algorithm 2
09  sum = (start + end)*(end - start + 1)/2
10  print("Algorithm 2: sum = ",sum)
```

16. Give **three** advantages of using subroutines in programs. [3]

TOPICS FOR PAPER 2
COMPUTING CONCEPTS

Information about Paper 2

Written exam: 1 hour 45 minutes
90 marks
50% of GCSE

Specification coverage

Fundamentals of data representation, computer systems, fundamentals of computer networks, cyber security, relational databases and structured query language (SQL).

Ethical, legal and environmental impacts of digital technology on wider society, including issues of privacy.

The content for this assessment will be drawn from subject content sections 3.3 to 3.8 of the specification.

Questions

A mix of multiple choice, short answer, longer answer and extended response questions assessing SQL programming skills and theoretical knowledge.

NUMBER BASES

Units of data storage

| Bit
0 or 1 | Nibble
4 Bits | Byte
8 Bits | Kilobyte
1000 Bytes | Megabyte
1000 kB | Gigabyte
1000 MB | Terabyte
1000 GB | Petabyte
1000 TB |

Switches

A computer is made up of billions of **switches**, each with two states - an off position (represented by a 0) and an on position (represented by a 1). This is known as **binary**. All data therefore needs to be converted into binary before it can be processed by a computer.

By placing two or more switches in a row, you double the number of combinations of 1s and 0s with each additional switch.

Work out the following:

(a) Calculate the number of 650 MB CDs required to store 2 GB of images. Show your working. [1]

(b) Calculate the total capacity of a server with 4 x 2.5 TB hard disk drives. [1]

(c) Calculate the total storage requirement for a database of 5,000 customer records each of 1.5 kB each. Give your answer in MB. Show your working. [2]

(a) 2 GB = 2000 MB. 2000/650 = 3.08 (>3). Therefore 4 CDs will be required.[1]

(b) 10 TB[1]

(c) 5000 × 1.5 kB = 7500 kB[1] = 7.5 MB.[1]

Look at a variety of on / off (1 or 0) switches on electrical items.

What do you think this symbol represents?

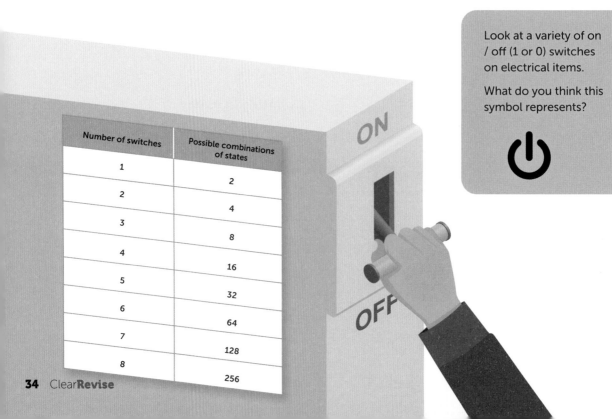

Number of switches	Possible combinations of states
1	2
2	4
3	8
4	16
5	32
6	64
7	128
8	256

BINARY ⇄ DECIMAL CONVERSION

Converting binary numbers into positive decimal whole numbers

Our **decimal** or **denary** system has a base of 10 digits 0–9. Binary has a **base** of just 2 digits, 0 and 1. Instead of a representing three-digit numbers with a ones, tens and hundreds column for example, binary represents them with a ones column, a twos column and a fours column.

To make a conversion from binary to decimal, add the place value headers where there is a 1.

128	64	32	16	8	4	2	1
0	1	1	0	1	0	0	1
	1×64 +	1×32 +		1×8 +			1×1 = 105

Converting positive decimal whole numbers to binary

To convert the decimal number 87 into binary, start with the **most significant bit** (left-hand end of the table below). Does 128 go into 87? If not, add a 0 in that column. Does 64 go into 87? Yes, it does, so add a 1 to the column and calculate the remainder, 23. 32 does not go into 23 so add a 0 to the next column. 16 goes into 23 with a remainder of 7. 8 won't go into 7 so add a 0 next. 4 will go with a remainder of 3. 2 will go into 3 with a remainder of 1 and 1 goes into 1 so add a 1 to each of the last three columns.

Note that the maximum value that can be held in eight bits where all bits are equal to 1, is 255.

A binary number with a 1 in the least significant bit (far right-hand position) will always be odd.

128	64	32	16	8	4	2	1
0	1	0	1	0	1	1	1
	r23		r7		r3	r1	r0

1. Convert the following decimal numbers to binary:
   (a) 138 [1]
   (b) 57 [1]
2. Convert the following binary numbers to decimal:
   (a) 0110 1101 [1]
   (b) 1110 0110 [1]

1. (a) 1000 1010[1], (b) 0011 1001[1]
2. (a) 109[1], (b) 230[1]

Counting in binary

0	0000		8	1000
1	0001		9	1001
2	0010		10	1010
3	0011		11	1011
4	0100		12	1100
5	0101		13	1101
6	0110		14	1110
7	0111		15	1111

HEXADECIMAL ⇄ BINARY CONVERSION

The **hexadecimal** number system uses a base of 16 instead of 2 or 10. Given that we only have ten digits 0–9 in our system, the additional six numbers 10–15 in the hexadecimal system are represented by the letters A–F.

Decimal	Binary	Hex		Decimal	Binary	Hex
0	0000	0		8	1000	8
1	0001	1		9	1001	9
2	0010	2		10	1010	A
3	0011	3		11	1011	B
4	0100	4		12	1100	C
5	0101	5		13	1101	D
6	0110	6		14	1110	E
7	0111	7		15	1111	F

One hexadecimal (or hex) number can represent one nibble of 4 bits. For this reason, it is easier to remember hexadecimal numbers than binary ones.

Converting a binary number into hexadecimal

To convert the number 0100 1111 to hexadecimal, first split the eight-bit binary number into two nibbles of four bits each. Convert each nibble separately and join the results.

0100	1111		01001111
4	15 (F)	=	4F

Some further examples are:
1011 0101 = **B5** and 1100 1101 = **CD**

Converting a hexadecimal number into binary

Convert each hex character into a four-bit binary value and join them to make a byte.

7	E (14)		7E
0111	1110	=	01111110

Further examples are: B9 = 1011 1001 and DA = 1101 1010.

1. Convert the following binary values into hexadecimal: [3]
   (a) 0110 1011
   (b) 0000 1001
   (c) 1111 1111

2. Convert the following hexadecimal values into binary: [2]
   (a) 48
   (b) 6A
   (c) F9

1. (a) 6B[1], (b) 09[1], (c) FF[1]
2. (a) 0100 1000[1],
   (b) 0110 1010[1],
   (c) 1111 1001[1]

HEXADECIMAL ⇄ DECIMAL CONVERSION

To convert between **hexadecimal** and **decimal**, you need to remember that hex has a base of 16, as opposed to our decimal number system that has a base of 10. This means that instead of 1s and 10s, you have 1s and 16s.

Converting a hexadecimal number into decimal

Multiply the hexadecimal digits by their column place values 16 and 1, then add the results.

To convert the hex number 5B to decimal:

16	1	
5	B	(B = 11)
(5 × 16)	(11 × 1)	
80	11	80 + 11 = 91

Here are some further examples:
Hexadecimal 88 = decimal **136** and hexadecimal FA = decimal **250**

Converting a decimal number into hexadecimal

First work out how many 16s go into the number. This is the first hex digit. Then take the remainder and use this as the second hex digit. To convert 195 to hex:

195 / 16 = 12 remainder 3
12 = **C**
3 = **3**   so 195 in decimal is
       C3 in hexadecimal

Here are some further examples:
Decimal 67 = hexadecimal **43**
Decimal 219 = hexadecimal **DB**

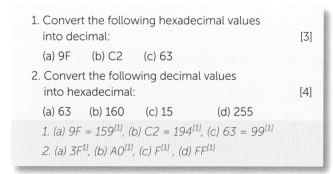

1. Convert the following hexadecimal values into decimal: [3]
   (a) 9F   (b) C2   (c) 63
2. Convert the following decimal values into hexadecimal: [4]
   (a) 63   (b) 160   (c) 15   (d) 255

1. (a) 9F = 159[1], (b) C2 = 194[1], (c) 63 = 99[1]
2. (a) 3F[1], (b) A0[1], (c) F[1], (d) FF[1]

USES OF HEXADECIMAL

Hexadecimal numbers are easier to read and remember than binary so they are used to represent the following:

- Colour values in photo editing software and HTML
- MAC addresses
- Memory address locations in assembly language

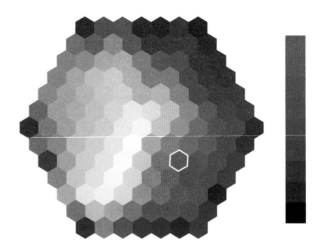

Hexadecimal colour number: ED468C

BINARY ARITHMETIC

Binary addition is done in the same way that decimal numbers might be added together.

The rules are as follows:

0 + 0 = 0

0 + 1 or 1 + 0 = 1

1 + 1 = 0 carry 1

1 + 1 + 1 = 1 carry 1

To add three binary numbers, add the first two, then add the third to the result.

Carry	1	1	1	1		1			Check
	0	1	0	1	1	0	1	1	91
+	0	0	1	1	1	0	1	0	58
1	**0**	**0**	**1**	**0**	**1**	**0**	**1**		**149**

Calculate the total of the following binary numbers, giving your answer in binary.

    (a) 0011 1011 + 1000 0110   [1]

    (b) 0010 0110 + 0001 1110 + 0001 1100   [2]

(a) 1100 0001[1], (b) 0110 0000[1] and workings. [1]

Note that in the same way as the decimal values 00028 and 28 represent the same value, the binary value 00011100 is the same as 11100. Any zeros before the most significant bit (left-hand side) are ignored.

BINARY SHIFTS

A **binary shift** moves all of the bits in a given binary number either to the left or the right by a given number of places. All of the empty spaces are then filled with zeros.

A shift of one place to the left will have the following effect:

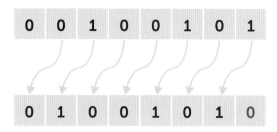

Effects of shifts

A shift to the left will multiply a binary number by 2. Two shifts left would therefore multiply a number by 4. Each shift right would divide a number by 2. Similarly, moving the decimal number 17 one place left becomes 170 and has therefore been multiplied by its base of 10.

An issue with precision occurs where odd numbers are divided since a standard byte cannot represent fractional numbers. Consider the following shift of three places to the right:

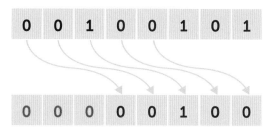

The original binary value was equal to decimal 37. A right shift should divide this by 8 (or divide by 2, three times). 37 / 8 = 4.625. However, the resulting binary converted to decimal is 4.

---

1. Complete a 2-place shift to the right on the binary number 11010110. [1]
2. Explain the effect of performing a right shift of two places on the binary number 11010110. [2]
3. Explain the effect of performing a left shift of 1 place on the binary number 11010110. [2]

1. *0011 0101[1]*

2. *Each shift right will divide the number by 2, so a two-place shift right will divide the number by 4[1]. However, if the shift results in one or more 1s being lost at the right hand end, the results will lose precision[1]. This is demonstrated in this question. 1101 0110 is 214 in decimal. Dividing that by 4 = 53.5. The shifted result, 0011 0101, however, is only 53 in decimal.*

3. *Shifting one place left multiplies the number by 2.[1] However this will cause an overflow error[1] for the given number, as 9 bits would be needed for the result[1], which will not fit in 1 byte[1].*

CHARACTER ENCODING

Each **character** on a keyboard has a binary code which is transmitted to the computer each time a key is pressed. Some of the characters and their codes, known as the **character set**, for the standard keyboard are given below. The **ASCII** character set consists of 128 characters, each using 7 bits to uniquely represent them. ASCII stands for American Standard Code for Information Interchange.

7-bit ASCII table

ASCII	DEC	Binary	ASCII	DEC	Binary	ASCII	DEC	Binary	ASCII	DEC	Binary
NULL	000	000 0000	space	032	010 0000	@	064	100 0000	`	096	110 0000
SOH	001	000 0001	!	033	010 0001	A	065	100 0001	a	097	110 0001
STX	002	000 0010	"	034	010 0010	B	066	100 0010	b	098	110 0010
ETX	003	000 0011	#	035	010 0011	C	067	100 0011	c	099	110 0011
EOT	004	000 0100	$	036	010 0100	D	068	100 0100	d	100	110 0100
ENQ	005	000 0101	%	037	010 0101	E	069	100 0101	e	101	110 0101
ACK	006	000 0110	&	038	010 0110	F	070	100 0110	f	102	110 0110
BEL	007	000 0111	'	039	010 0111	G	071	100 0111	g	103	110 0111
BS	008	000 1000	(	040	010 1000	H	072	100 1000	h	104	110 1000
HT	009	000 1001	)	041	010 1001	I	073	100 1001	i	105	110 1001
LF	010	000 1010	*	042	010 1010	J	074	100 1010	j	106	110 1010
VT	011	000 1011	+	043	010 1011	K	075	100 1011	k	107	110 1011
FF	012	000 1100	,	044	010 1100	L	076	100 1100	l	108	110 1100
CR	013	000 1101	-	045	010 1101	M	077	100 1101	m	109	110 1101
SO	014	000 1110	.	046	010 1110	N	078	100 1110	n	110	110 1110
SI	015	000 1111	/	047	010 1111	O	079	100 1111	o	111	110 1111
DLE	016	001 0000	0	048	011 0000	P	080	101 0000	p	112	111 0000
DC1	017	001 0001	1	049	011 0001	Q	081	101 0001	q	113	111 0001
DC2	018	001 0010	2	050	011 0010	R	082	101 0010	r	114	111 0010
DC3	019	001 0011	3	051	011 0011	S	083	101 0011	s	115	111 0011
DC4	020	001 0100	4	052	011 0100	T	084	101 0100	t	116	111 0100
NAK	021	001 0101	5	053	011 0101	U	085	101 0101	u	117	111 0101
SYN	022	001 0110	6	054	011 0110	V	086	101 0110	v	118	111 0110
ETB	023	001 0111	7	055	011 0111	W	087	101 0111	w	119	111 0111
CAN	024	001 1000	8	056	011 1000	X	088	101 1000	x	120	111 1000
EM	025	001 1001	9	057	011 1001	Y	089	101 1001	y	121	111 1001
SUB	026	001 1010	:	058	011 1010	Z	090	101 1010	z	122	111 1010
ESC	027	001 1011	;	059	011 1011	[	091	101 1011	{	123	111 1011
FS	028	001 1100	<	060	011 1100	\	092	101 1100			124	111 1100
GS	029	001 1101	=	061	011 1101	]	093	101 1101	}	125	111 1101
RS	030	001 1110	>	062	011 1110	^	094	101 1110	~	126	111 1110
US	031	001 1111	?	063	011 1111	_	095	101 1111	DEL	127	111 1111

Using the ASCII table in programming

The character codes are grouped and run in sequence; e.g. given that uppercase 'A' is 65 then 'B' must be 66 and so on. The pattern applies to other groupings such as lowercase characters and digits. For example, '1' is 49, so '5' must be 53. Also, '3' < '4' and 'a' < 'b'.

Notice that the ASCII code value for '7' (011 0111) is different from the pure binary value for 7 (000 0111). This is why you can't calculate with numbers that have been input as strings.

Character sets

A character set consists of all the letters, numbers and special characters that can be recognised by a computer system. The ASCII character set uses 7 bits and consists of 128 characters as shown in the table opposite.

Extended ASCII

Extended ASCII uses 8 bits rather than 7. This allows up to 256 characters to be represented. Additional characters in the set include symbols, common foreign language characters and mathematical characters for example, ©, €, é and ¼. 7-bit codes translate into 8-bit codes directly using an additional 0 as the most significant (leftmost) bit. For example, 'a' translates from 110 0001 to 0110 0001.

Unicode

Unicode uses 16 bits per character, and can represent 65,536 different characters. This is enough to represent the characters in most international languages including those in Russian, Chinese, Arabic and emojis ☺. Unicode uses the same codes as ASCII up to 127.

Use the ASCII table for this question.

(a) Show how the word CAGE is represented in 8-bit ASCII.
  Give your answer in binary. [1]

(b) State how many bytes would be used to store the phrase "BIRD CAGE" using extended 8-bit ASCII. [1]

(c) The uppercase character 'T' in ASCII is represented by the decimal value 84.
  State the decimal value for the character 'R'. [1]

(a) Each letter would be represented in one byte by its binary ASCII value written in the same order that the characters are entered, e.g.
  01000011 01000001 01000111 01000101[1]

(b) 9 bytes.[1] (The Space character has the code 32 and occupies one byte.)

(c) 'R' is 82.[1]

REPRESENTING IMAGES

Similar to a mosaic, a **bitmap** image is made up of picture elements or **pixels**. A pixel represents the smallest identifiable area of an image, each appearing as a square of a single colour.

Image size

The size of an image is expressed as width × height of the image in pixels, for example 600 × 400px.

Number of colours		Colour depth
2 colours	2^1 colours	1 bit per pixel required
4 colours	2^2 colours	2 bits per pixel required
8 colours	2^3 colours	3 bits per pixel required
16 colours	2^4 colours	4 bits per pixel required

Colour depth

The first symbol below is represented in black and white using a series of binary codes. 0 = black and 1 = white.

0	1	1	1
1	0	1	0
1	1	0	0
1	0	0	0

11	11	11	00
10	10	10	10
10	10	01	10
10	10	01	10

Given that only 1 bit per pixel is available, only two colours, black and white, can be represented. The full image would have a size of 16 bits or 2 bytes. If the number of bits per pixel is increased, more colours can be represented. In the second example, four colours can be represented as the **colour depth** (also known as **bit depth**), or bits per pixel has been doubled to two. This will also double the file size.

1. Study the bitmap images above.

   (a) Give the binary representation for the top row of the 4-colour example. [2]

   (b) State the colour depth of an image if a palette of 256 colours per pixel is required. [1]

   The number of available colours in the 4 x 4 pixel image above is increased to 256.

   (c) State the effect on the file size of the image. [1]

   (a) 11 11[1] 11 00[1]. One mark per correct pair.

   (b) 8 bits per pixel.[1] (2^8 = 256)

   (c) The file size would increase[1] to 1 byte per pixel, i.e. 16 bytes for the whole image[1].

Effect of colour depth and resolution

As the number of bits per pixel increases (the **colour depth** or **bit depth**), so does the quality of the image as you are able to more accurately represent the full range of colours visible to the naked eye. However, this significantly increases the **file size**.

| 2 colours | 4 colours | 8 colours | 16 colours | 256 colours | 65.536 colours | 16.7m colours |

The file size of an image in bits can be calculated as *width in pixels x height in pixels x colour depth*. Dividing by 8 will give the size in bytes.

Simply increasing the number of pixels in an image will also increase its size. An 8 x 8 pixel icon will be four times larger than a 4 x 4 pixel icon with the same colour depth.

| 1 x 1 | 2 x 2 | 5 x 5 | 10 x 10 | 25 x 25 | 50 x 50 | 72 x 72 | 300 x 300 |

The density of pixels in the same sized area defines the **resolution**. More pixels per inch (**PPI**) will smooth the edges and improve the overall quality. This will increase the size of the image file, making it possible to enlarge the image without a visible loss of quality. Improved resolution, however, comes at the expense of either increasing the number of pixels in an image (increasing file size) or reducing the pixel size and therefore the visible size of the image.

2. An image has 1000 x 1000 pixels and a colour depth of 24 bits.

    (a) State the file size of the image in MB. [2]

    (b) Calculate how many colours are available for each pixel if an image has a colour depth of 8 bits. [1]

    (a) 3 MB.[1] *1000 x 1000 * 24 / 8 = 3,000 kB*[1] *or 3 MB.*

    (b) 2^8 = 256 colours.[1]

REPRESENTING SOUND

Analogue sounds must be digitally recorded in binary. In order to record sound, the **amplitude** or height of the soundwave emitted must be measured and recorded at regular intervals. How often the height is recorded (the **frequency** or **sampling rate**), and the accuracy to which the height is recorded (the **bit depth** or **sample resolution**) affect the quality of the recorded sound when played back and the file size of the recording. The **duration** of the recording will also affect the file size.

The **sampling rate** is measured in **hertz**. CD quality playback is recorded at 44.1 kHz.

Examples A and B show how the digitally represented wave more accurately follows the analogue sound wave form with a greater **bit depth**.

Examples B and C show how a wave recorded at identical resolution is much more accurately represented with a greater number of **samples per second**.

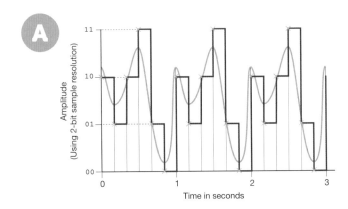

Look at Examples A, B and C.

(a) Give the binary representation for the first six samples taken in the first second of recording in Example A. [2]

(b) State how many different amplitudes or wave heights could be recorded if the bit depth was 8. [1]

(c) State the sample frequency in hertz of Example C. [1]

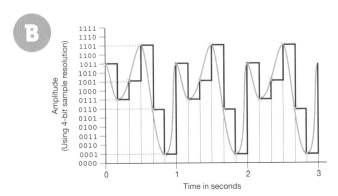

(d) Calculate the file size in bytes of a message alert tone lasting 3 seconds, using a sampling rate of 8 kHz and an 8-bit sample resolution. [1]

(a) 10, 01, 10[1], 11, 01, 00[1]

(b) $2^8 = 256$[1]

(c) 3 Hz[1] (3 samples per second.)

(d) 8,000 samples per second, taken at 8 bits each = 64 kilobits / 8 = 8 kB x 3 seconds duration = 24 kB.[1]

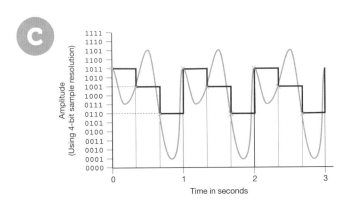

DATA COMPRESSION

Compression software uses **algorithms** to remove repeated or unnecessary data. This reduces the size of a file on disk, and of large files sent by email where there are maximum attachment limits. It is also useful for streaming data over the Internet and for images and video embedded within websites as smaller files will be transmitted in less time, meaning the streamed video content or website takes less time to download. A **bitmap** (**.bmp**) image is uncompressed.

Type	Lossy compression	Lossless compression
Formats	JPG, MP3, WMV, MPG	TIF, PDF, GIF, PNG, MOV, ZIP
Examples		
Advantages	Smallest file sizes, least transmission time, reduces Internet traffic and collisions	Original quality is preserved / no information or data is lost
Disadvantages	Detail is permanently lost	Less significant reduction in file size
Example uses	Music streaming, online images and video, image libraries on devices or in the cloud	Text documents, electronic books, high resolution print documents

1. A large software program is being distributed via an online download.
   (a) Give **two** advantages of using compression software for online downloads. [2]
   (b) Explain which type of compression should be used to compress the software. [2]

   (a) Smaller size on the server[1], reduces download time because it is a smaller file size[1], reduces Internet traffic[1], uses less download data for users on a limited tariff[1].

   (b) Lossless compression[1] software must be used as no data in the software program can be lost[1]. Lost data would prevent the software from running once uncompressed[1].

Run length encoding (RLE)

Data, particularly image data, can be represented using frequency/data pairs. For example, a black and white 5x5 image with a colour depth of 1 may be represented by the binary string: 0000011100000111100. This could be represented saying "five zeros, three ones" and so on or using **RLE** as 50 31 50 51 20.

2. Write out the bit pattern for the following RLE encoded data: 40 31 30 21 [2]

   0000 111[1] 000 11[1]

HUFFMAN CODING

Huffman coding is a compression technique for reducing the number of bits used to represent each character in a body of text.

The more frequently a character appears, the fewer bits are used to represent it and the higher up the Huffman tree (see below) it will appear.

Example

Consider the sentence: **EVIL RATS STEAL LIVE PET**. The frequency that each letter in the sentence appears is first recorded in a table.

Character	Space	E	L	V	I	A	T	S	R	P
Frequency	4	4	3	2	2	2	2	2	1	1
	00	10	010	0110	0111	1100	1101	1110	11110	11111

A tree is then formed using the most frequent letters nearer the top of the tree. In the exam, you will only be required to interpret a tree. You will not need to build one.

Using this tree, each character code is derived from the route taken to it. Left is 0, right is 1. 'A' is therefore represented as right, right, left, left or 1100. The word 'RAIL' would be encoded as 11110 1100 0111 010. This is 16 bits or 2 bytes. In ASCII, 'RAIL' would be stored as 4 bytes so the data compressed by the Huffman coding represents a 50% reduction in size.

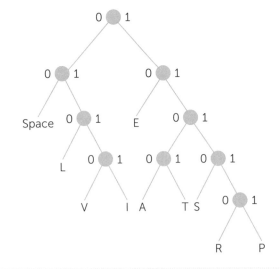

This question uses the Huffman tree given above.

(a) State the coding for the word LET. [3]

(b) Calculate how many bits these three letters would require using the Huffman code. [1]

(c) The sentence EVIL RATS STEAL LIVE PET is represented in a total of 79 bits.
    Calculate how many bytes would be required to represent the sentence using 8-bit ASCII. [1]

(d) Calculate how many bits are saved by compressing the sentence using Huffman coding instead of ASCII. [2]

(a) 010[1], 10[1], 1101[1]

(b) 3 + 2 + 4 = 9 bits[1]

(c) 24 bytes[1]

(d) 24 bytes * 8 bits / byte = 192 bits[1]. 192 - 79 = 113 bits[1] saved.

EXAMINATION PRACTICE

1. Calculate the following:
   (a) The number of bytes in a 4.5 kB text document.   [1]
   (b) The number of Megabytes in a 2 GB sound recording.   [1]
   (c) The decimal number 28 can be represented in binary using 8 bits.
       (i) Convert decimal 28 to binary.   [1]
       (ii) Explain how a binary shift could be used to divide the binary number 01110100 by 2. [2]

2. Standard SMS text message technology permits 160 characters per message using the
   8-bit ASCII character set.
   (a) Explain what is meant by 'character set'.   [1]
   (b) Using this technology, state how many bytes are used to send a message of 160 characters
       in 16-bit Unicode.   [1]
   (c) The character representing 'Hi' in Chinese, Japanese and Korean (CJK) is 嗨.
       The Unicode hexadecimal character code for 嗨 is 55E8.
       (i) Complete the hexadecimal conversion of 55E8 into binary below.   [2]

Hex:	5	5	E	8
Binary:	0101	0101		

       (ii) Explain why smartphones that can send text messages in multiple languages would use
            Unicode instead of ASCII as their character set.   [2]

3. A bitmap image with a colour depth of 1 bit has been created.
   (a) Convert the following binary data into an image with a resolution of 5 x 5 pixels, where 0
       represents black and 1 represents white:
       00100 10101 10001 00000 10101   [3]
   (b) The first five bits of the image are 00100. Show how these might be compressed in data/
       frequency pairs using run length encoding (RLE).   [1]
   (c) Justify an appropriate compression method for an image designed for use on a website.   [4]

4. Anil has made a sound recording of a short piece of music. The quality of the playback is poor.
   Anil believes this is to do with the sample resolution.
   (a) State what is meant by 'sample resolution'.   [1]
   (b) Explain how the sample resolution could affect the quality of a sound recording.   [2]

   Anil says that the file size of the recording needs to be below his email attachment limit.

   (c) Describe **one** factor besides sample resolution which will affect the file size of Anil's recording. [2]

5. Describe how Huffman coding can be used to compress a text file.   [4]

HARDWARE AND SOFTWARE

A computer system is made up of **hardware** and **software**. Hardware is any physical component that makes up a computer. Software is any program that runs on the computer. You can touch hardware. You cannot touch software.

Computer systems are all around us. They are not just the PCs on the desk but include mobile phones, cash machines, supermarket tills and the engine management systems in a modern-day car.

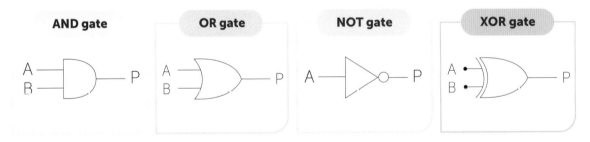

3.4.2

BOOLEAN LOGIC

Simple logic gates

Computers are made of **logic gates**, **transistors** and **switches** which can be in one of two states: on or off, 1 or 0. You need to know about four simple logic gates that are used in electronics. Each is represented by a diagram and a truth table showing the possible outputs for each possible input.

AND gate	**OR gate**	**NOT gate**	**XOR gate**

AND			OR			NOT		XOR		
A	B	P = A AND B	A	B	P = A OR B	A	P = NOT A	A	B	P = A XOR B
0	0	0	0	0	0	0	1	0	0	0
0	1	0	0	1	1	1	0	0	1	1
1	0	0	1	0	1			1	0	1
1	1	1	1	1	1			1	1	0

An XOR gate represents the **exclusive OR**. The output is True, or 1, when either input is 1, but not when both inputs are 1.

CONSTRUCTING LOGIC CIRCUITS

Boolean expression symbols

Each gate has a specific symbol which is used to represent it in an expression.

- AND is represented by •
- OR is represented by +
- NOT is represented by using an overbar, e.g.: 'Not A' would be written as $\overline{A}$
- XOR is represented by $\oplus$

Combining gates in circuits

Logic gates can be combined to produce more complicated circuits. This circuit can be represented by the **logic statement**: P = (A AND B) OR (NOT B), written as P = (A • B) + $\overline{B}$.

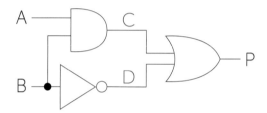

The truth table is given below.

A	B	C (A AND B)	D (NOT B)	P (C OR D)
0	0	0	1	1
0	1	0	0	0
1	0	0	1	1
1	1	1	0	1

1. Below is a logic diagram.

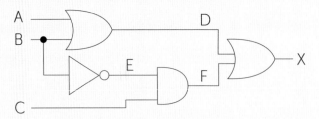

(a) Write the logic statements for D and E. [2]

(b) Write the logic statement corresponding to the logic diagram, in terms of inputs A, B and C and output X. Show your working. [4]

2. Draw a logic diagram for the expression $P = ((\overline{A + B})) \oplus C$. [3]

3. A logic circuit is being developed for a bus shelter advert that plays automatically if a passenger is detected in or around the bus stop.

- The system has two sensors, S1 and S2, that detect if a passenger is near. The advert plays if either of these sensors is activated.

- The system should only play if it is not daytime (D).

- The output from the circuit, for whether the advert should play or not, is P.

Draw the logic circuit for this system. [3]

1. (a) D = A OR B[1], E = NOT B[1], or D = A + B[1], E = $\overline{B}$ [1]

(b) X = D OR F[1] or X = D + F[1]

$\quad$ = (A OR B) OR (C AND E)[1] or (A + B) + (C • E)[1]

$\quad$ = (A OR B)[1] OR (C AND NOT B)[1] or (A + B)[1] + (C • $\overline{B}$)[1]

2. One mark[1] for each correct gate.

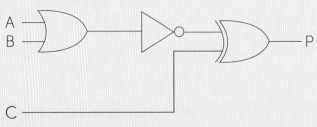

3. One mark[1] for each correct gate.

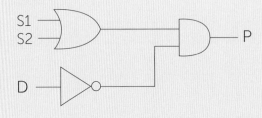

OPERATING SYSTEMS

System software programs are those that are needed to enable the computer to function, including the operating system (OS), utilities, library routines and programming language translators.

Major operating systems include **Windows®**, **Linux®**, **MacOS®**, Apple's **iOS®**, and Google's **Android®**.

The **operating system** is a group of programs that is essential for managing the computer's resources. It manages five major areas:

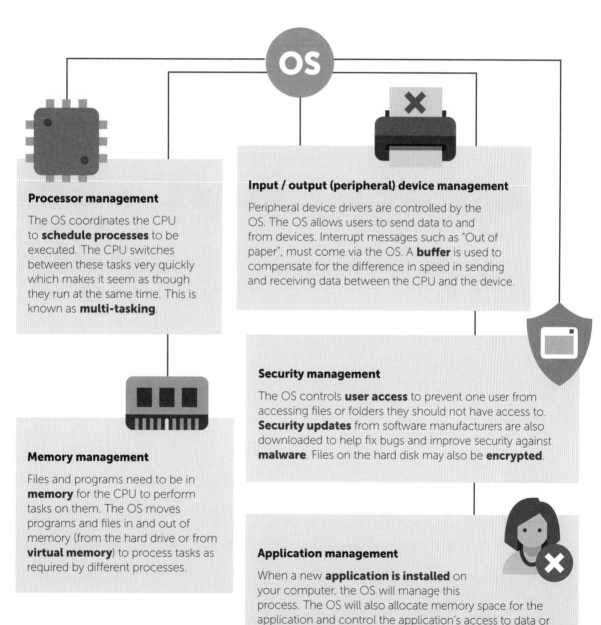

Processor management

The OS coordinates the CPU to **schedule processes** to be executed. The CPU switches between these tasks very quickly which makes it seem as though they run at the same time. This is known as **multi-tasking**.

Input / output (peripheral) device management

Peripheral device drivers are controlled by the OS. The OS allows users to send data to and from devices. Interrupt messages such as "Out of paper", must come via the OS. A **buffer** is used to compensate for the difference in speed in sending and receiving data between the CPU and the device.

Memory management

Files and programs need to be in **memory** for the CPU to perform tasks on them. The OS moves programs and files in and out of memory (from the hard drive or from **virtual memory**) to process tasks as required by different processes.

Security management

The OS controls **user access** to prevent one user from accessing files or folders they should not have access to. **Security updates** from software manufacturers are also downloaded to help fix bugs and improve security against **malware**. Files on the hard disk may also be **encrypted**.

Application management

When a new **application is installed** on your computer, the OS will manage this process. The OS will also allocate memory space for the application and control the application's access to data or devices. User access to programs is also managed.

UTILITY SOFTWARE

Utility programs are small programs that are used in conjunction with the main operating system in order to manage extra features or functions. They are not essential to the running of a computer but make specific tasks easier or add an additional layer of housekeeping.

Three common examples of utility program are:

Defragmentation software

Files are stored on the hard disk in blocks. As different sized files are added and deleted over time, gaps appear which may not fit all of the next file to be stored. Files therefore become fragmented in order to fit them in. Eventually the files need to be defragmented so that all the blocks for each file are together. A file saved in three fragments would take three times as long to find it all, so this process speeds up the computer's file retrieval and storage times.

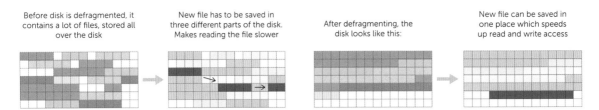

| Before disk is defragmented, it contains a lot of files, stored all over the disk | New file has to be saved in three different parts of the disk. Makes reading the file slower | After defragmenting, the disk looks like this: | New file can be saved in one place which speeds up read and write access |

Encryption software

Encryption utilities are used to encrypt or decrypt files or folders held on a computer, transmitted across a network or when they are transferred to external devices such as a USB flash drive. The encryption process uses an algorithm and a key to transform plaintext into ciphertext. To decode the original information (the plaintext), it would be necessary to know both the algorithm and the key.

Data compression software

Compression software (such as WinZip) uses an algorithm to resave the data in an existing file using less space than the original. Sometimes data is lost (lossy compression) and at other times, the file can still be reconstructed without any loss of information (lossless compression).

Compression software is a type of utility program.

(a) Explain **one** situation in which compression software would be useful. [2]

(b) Give **two** other examples of utility software. [2]

(a) When emailing files, compression software enables larger files to fit within email attachment limits[1], it reduces the data transfer volumes to meet ISP limits[1] and saves space on a local disk[1]. Compression software also allows multiple original files to be saved as one single file[1] which is helpful for email and distribution[1].

(b) Encryption software[1], defragmentation software[1], backup utilities[1], anti-virus or anti-spyware software[1], software firewalls[1], auto-update utilities[1] and disk formatting software[1].

APPLICATION SOFTWARE

Application software is for computer users to enable them to perform specific tasks such as word processing, graphic design or program development.

Examples of application software include the **Microsoft Office** suite, **payroll systems**, **school registration** and **tracking systems** and **smartphone applications**.

1. Describe **one** difference between application software and system software. [2]

   Application software provides a means for users to complete tasks[1]. System software manages the hardware and the software being executed on the computer or system[1].

2. Complete the table below. The first line is completed for you. [7]

Software	Software type	Typical task
Word processing	Application	Edit a document
SatNav software		
		Allocates memory to a program in a multi-tasking system
I/O management		
Anti-virus software		
	Application	Enables users to access websites and display web content
		Schedules processes in a multi-tasking environment
Compiler		

Software	Software type	Typical task
Word processing	Application	Edit a document
SatNav software	Application	Calculate the distance from current location to a destination/plan the quickest or best route/advise on traffic holdups[1]
Memory management	System[1]	Allocates memory to a program in a multi-tasking system
I/O management	System	Coordinates the flow of traffic between internal resources and external devices /reports on device status/responds to messages (e.g. "print job completed" or "out of paper" sent from printer[1]
Anti-virus software	Utility	Identifies and removes computer viruses[1]
Web browser[1]	Application	Enables users to access websites and display web content
Processor management	System[1]	Schedules processes in a multi-tasking environment
Compiler	System[1]	Translates the source code written by a programmer into executable machine code

CLASSIFICATION OF PROGRAMMING LANGUAGES

High- and low-level programming languages

A **high-level language** has a **syntax** and structure similar to **English** that is designed to be understood by humans. Most programs are written in high-level languages for this reason.

For example:
```
speed = distance / time
print(speed)
```

Python, Visual Basic and C# are examples of high-level languages. These are hardware independent, meaning they can run on any system. The programmer can therefore concentrate on their own task rather than concerning themselves with the architecture of the computer.

High-level code must be **compiled** or **interpreted** before it can be run.

Source code
Written in a high-level language → **Compiler** → **Object code** (machine code)

Assembly language is a **low-level language** which is typically used to control specific hardware components. Low-level commands execute very quickly. Software for embedded systems is often written in assembly language, because the machine code produced by the assembler is fast, efficient and occupies less memory than that produced by translating the equivalent high-level instructions.

Machine code and assembly language

Processors execute machine code, the binary instructions which the computer can respond to directly to perform a task. Each type of processor has its own specific machine code instruction set so machine code produced for one type will not work on another.

A programmer is writing a revision app for a mobile phone. The program is written in a high-level code and then translated to machine code.

Describe **two** differences between high-level code and machine code. [4]

High-level code has English-like structures such as IF...THEN...ELSE, WHILE...ENDWHILE.[1] It uses complex conditional statements and identifiers using an unlimited number of characters.[1] It has data structures such as arrays[1] which are either unavailable or much easier to use than in a low-level language.[1]

Machine code has statements which can manipulate specific hardware components.[1]

High-level language programs are easier to learn.[1] Programs written in high-level languages are also quicker to write[1] and easier to maintain[1].

TRANSLATORS

There are three common types of translator: a **compiler**, an **interpreter** and an **assembler**. These work in different ways, each having different advantages.

Compiler	Interpreter
Translates a high-level language program (source code) in one go to produce object code	Translates and executes one line of a high-level language program at a time
A compiled program executes faster as it is already in machine code	Takes more time to execute as each instruction is translated before it is executed
Produces an executable file so the original code does not need to be compiled again	Original code will be interpreted or translated every time it is run
No need for the compiler to be present when the object code is run	The interpreter must be installed to run the program

1. Describe the need for a translator when using a high-level language. [2]

A translator (compiler or interpreter) converts high-level code into machine code or binary instructions[1] to enable the code to be run[1].

Assembler

An assembler converts assembly language into machine code. This is a simple conversion as, in general, every assembly language instruction is translated into a single machine code instruction.

Example: The assembly code instruction LDA #17 loads the value 17 into the accumulator.

The assembler translates this into the machine code instruction, e.g. 11010100 00010001.

2. Techsoft is a software development company. The company has designed, developed and tested a new accounts package, suitable for small businesses. The package will be sold in the form of compiled object code.

Discuss why a compiler, rather than an interpreter, is used to translate the source code prior to selling the package software. [4]

A compiler will produce object code (machine code) which can be installed and executed[1], and this is the code that Techsoft will sell. The object code cannot be converted back to the original source code so there is no danger that their techniques will be copied and resold as original work.[1]

An interpreter does not produce object code which can be saved.[1] Techsoft would have to sell the source code, which could be copied or amended, possibly introducing errors. The interpreter (from a different company) would have to be installed on every computer using the software.[1] Each time the accounts software was run, the interpreter would be needed to translate each line of code into machine code and run it.[1]

SYSTEMS ARCHITECTURE

The purpose of the CPU

The purpose of the Central Processing Unit (CPU) is to continuously read and execute instructions stored in memory by repeatedly carrying out the fetch-execute cycle. The CPU contains the Arithmetic Logic Unit and the Control Unit, in addition to several general-purpose and special-purpose registers.

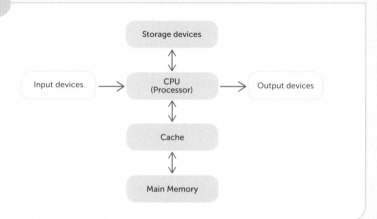

A single 4.5 GHz processor has 4,500,000,000 clock cycles or 'ticks' a second. This is known as the clock speed.

The fetch-execute cycle

Every CPU instruction is fetched from memory. Once fetched, it is decoded by the Control Unit to find out what to do with it. Then the instruction is executed. Every operation carried out within the fetch-execute cycle is regulated by a 'tick' or cycle of the CPU clock.

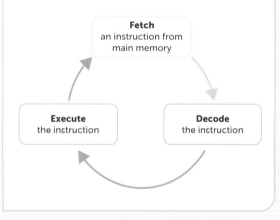

List **two** input devices and **one** output device that may be connected to the CPU. [3]

Input devices include a keyboard[1], mouse[1], scanner[1], microphone[1] and web cam[1]. Output devices include a monitor[1], printer[1] and speaker[1].

COMMON CPU COMPONENTS AND THEIR FUNCTION

CPU component	Function
ALU (Arithmetic Logic Unit)	Carries out mathematical and logical operations including AND, OR and NOT, and binary shifts. It compares values held in registers
CU (Control Unit)	Coordinates all of the CPU's actions in the fetch-decode-execute cycle and decodes instructions. Sends and receives control signals to fetch and write data
Clock	The clock regulates the speed and timing of all signals and computer functions
Registers	Even smaller and faster than cache memory, registers are built into the CPU chip to temporarily store memory addresses, instructions or data. They are used in the fetch-execute cycle for specific purposes
Bus	A collection of wires used to transfer data and instructions from one component to another

Types of memory

There are three types of volatile memory. They all lose their contents when the power is switched off. **Main memory**, (or **RAM**), is largest. **Cache** is a more expensive, relatively small and fast memory that can transfer data to the CPU faster than RAM. It is used to hold recently used blocks of data or program instructions that are likely to be needed again. Some CPUs have different levels of cache with level 1 being the smallest and fastest. **Registers** are special-purpose memory locations located within the CPU, used in the execution of instructions. They are even smaller and faster than cache.

John von Neumann developed the **stored program computer**. The von Neumann architecture involves storing both programs and the data they use in memory.

Explain how increased cache memory can improve the performance of the Central Processing Unit (CPU). [2]

Frequently used data or instructions are stored in cache[1] so that the CPU does not need to fetch them from RAM[1]. Cache is quicker for the CPU to access than RAM.[1]

CPU PERFORMANCE

Clock speed

The **clock speed** determines the number of **fetch-execute cycles** per second.
Every action taking place in the CPU takes place on a tick of the clock, or clock cycle. Each cycle is one **hertz** so a 3.7 GHz processor will cycle at 3.7 billion times per second.

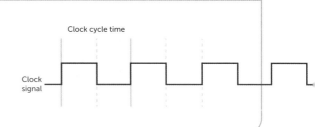

Clock cycle time

Clock signal

Cache size

Since **cache memory** operates much faster than main memory, data is transferred in and out of cache memory more quickly, which makes the CPU more efficient as less time is spent waiting for data to be transferred. There are two or three levels of cache. The fastest cache with the smallest capacity is Level 1 cache. The CPU will optimise its use of the fastest cache before using the next level, or using **Random Access Memory** (**RAM**), in order to improve performance speed.

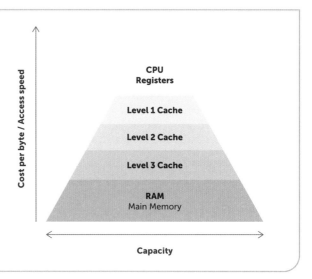

Cost per byte / Access speed

CPU Registers

Level 1 Cache

Level 2 Cache

Level 3 Cache

RAM
Main Memory

Capacity

Number of cores

A processor may contain more than one **core**. Each core can process one operation per clock cycle. A dual- or quad-core processor will be able to perform 2 or 4 operations simultaneously (for example, run two programs simultaneously), but only if the software it is running is designed for multi-core processors.

CPU

Dual Core

Quad Core

Octa Core

Amy's computer has a 4.5 GHz, dual core processor.

(a) How many cycles is a 4.5 GHz, dual core processor theoretically able to perform each second? [1]

(b) Explain why a computer with a dual core processor may not be twice as fast as a single core processor with the same clock speed. [2]

(a) 9 billion.[1]

(b) The software running on the computer may not be written to make the most efficient use of multiple cores.[1] Additional cores may be redundant if the software is only written for a single core[1] or if the output of one operation is required to perform the second operation[1] so they cannot be processed simultaneously[1].

MAIN MEMORY

Main memory (RAM or ROM) is directly accessible by the CPU. It is also known as primary storage.

The need for primary storage

RAM (**Random Access Memory**) is required to **temporarily store** the **programs**, **instructions** and **data** the computer needs whilst it is in operation. These are copied from the hard disk into main memory when they are required because it would be too slow to access everything directly from the hard disk. For even faster access, the most frequently used program instructions and data are held in **cache**.

RAM and ROM

RAM is the computer's temporary working memory. It is **volatile** which means it gets wiped as soon as the power is switched off. **ROM** (**Read Only Memory**) stores instructions and data that never need to be changed, such as the computer's start-up instructions so that it knows what to do when you push the 'on' button. ROM is **non-volatile**. As it is read-only, you cannot overwrite its contents once it has been set by the manufacturer.

RAM	ROM
Volatile – All data is lost when the power is turned off	Non-volatile – Data is permanently retained without power
Used as the computer's working memory for instructions, programs and data	Used for the computer's start-up instructions and in embedded systems
Can be written to, and read from	Read only, so cannot be written to

> 'Explain' questions such as 'Explain why this is the most appropriate...' are not just a list of benefits. You should identify the benefits but then expand on each one, whilst also applying it to the scenario or context in the question.

1. Abeel had a power cut whilst working on a spreadsheet document. He said that he lost the entire document but could still open the spreadsheet program when the power came back on.

   Explain why this was the case for Abeel. [2]

   The spreadsheet program was stored on the hard drive and copied to RAM / main memory while the program was in use.[1] The document was created and stored in RAM[1], and disappeared because it was never saved[1]. If the document had been saved, it would have been copied to the hard disk[1].

2. An increase in RAM capacity can improve the speed of your computer.

   Explain why an increase in ROM size would not have the same effect. [2]

   ROM is only required to be as large as the start-up instructions / BIOS inside it.[1] Any additional space will make no difference.[1] New files cannot be written into new space as it is read-only.[1]

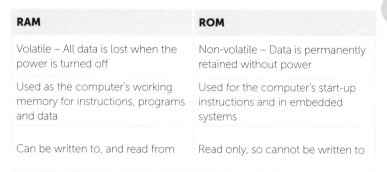

SECONDARY STORAGE

The need for secondary storage

Secondary storage includes **hard disks** (internal and external), **USB flash drives**, **CDs** and other portable storage devices. We need secondary storage for longer term storage of files and data because it is non-volatile, which means your data will not disappear when the power is turned off. External devices are portable and may have very large capacities.

The advantages and disadvantages of different storage devices

	Optical	Magnetic (HDD)	Solid state (SSD)
Capacity	From 650 MB (CD) to 50 GB (Blu-Ray Dual layer)	Up to 16 TB	Up to 4 TB for an SSD, or 256 GB for a USB flash drive
Speed	Up to 50 MB/s. Limited as there are moving parts	Up to 200 MB/s. Moving parts means relatively slow speed compared to SSD	Up to 3.5 GB/s for an SSD as there are no moving parts
Portability	Highly portable and lightweight	Internal drives are not portable. External drives are similar in size to a large smartphone	Flash drives and memory cards are highly portable. Internal SSDs are not intended to be portable but are very lightweight for use in laptops and tablet computers
Durability	Susceptible to scratches and will degrade over time and with exposure to sunlight	Good when not in use. Can be affected by magnetic fields and heat	Extremely durable
Reliability	Good in the medium term	Very reliable	Extremely reliable
Cost	50 GB for 45p	8 TB for £120	4 TB for £400

When asked questions that require a choice of storage, justify each choice on grounds of two or three of the characteristics: capacity, speed, portability, durability, reliability and cost.

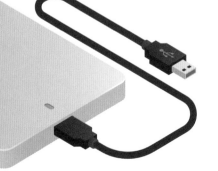

1. Explain why secondary storage is necessary in most smartphones. [2]
2. Explain why a solid state drive is commonly chosen for smartphone storage. [4]

1. *Secondary storage is non-volatile.[1] Without secondary storage, you are not able to store photos, video and files for another session once the power has been switched off.[1]*

2. *Solid state storage is durable with no moving parts[1], so it will be more robust if dropped[1]. It is reliable which will mean few repairs or inconvenient faults.[1] It is portable and lightweight and takes up little physical space[1], reducing the physical size of the device[1], ease of use[1] and weight[1] of the phone for the user. Solid state storage has very efficient power consumption[1] providing longer battery life for mobile devices[1].*

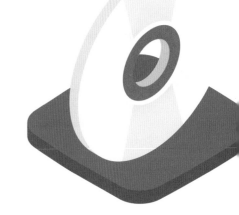

Applications of storage media

Solid state drives (SSDs) require very little power and create little heat owing to the lack of moving parts. This makes them suitable for laptop and tablet devices commonly used on the go. The lack of moving parts also means they are very small and reliable – perfect for small portable devices with built-in storage such as cameras and smartphones. SSDs are also used in desktop and larger computers and are replacing hard disks in mass storage facilities as they can be 100 times faster and do not require expensive cooling equipment.

Hard disk drives (HDDs) are commonly found in desktop computers, but SSDs are frequently used for some applications such as the operating system and other software that needs to execute as fast as possible. **CDs** and **DVDs** are useful for archiving data in the short to medium term given a life expectancy of 10–25 years. **USB flash drives** may be more effective for more regular backup of small files as they are more durable.

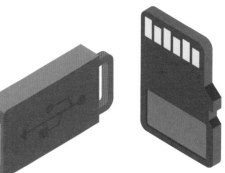

3. Justify a different storage device for each of the following applications.
   (a) A database server in a busy office. [3]
   (b) Event photographs sent by post to a company from a photographer. [3]
   (c) Regular transfer of files between home and a place of work. [3]

(a) Hard disk drives (HDD)[1] have very high capacities[1] and are relatively inexpensive compared to SSDs[1]. Fast, durable and reliable.[1] (Or, could justify SSD on grounds of speed, capacity, reliability.)

(b) CD or DVD.[1] Very inexpensive, costing only a few pence[1], easy to post[1], and will only be written to once[1].

(c) USB flash drive.[1] Has sufficient capacity and speed for this purpose[1], very portable[1], durable[1], reliable[1] and inexpensive[1]. (Accept valid alternatives.)

DEVICE OPERATION

Hard disk drives (HDD)

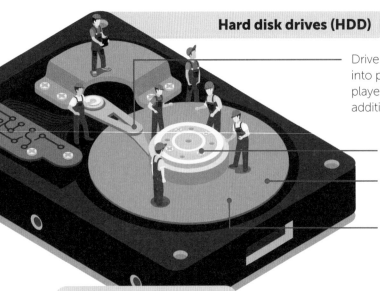

Drive read/write head moves into position, like a record player. This movement takes additional time.

Drive spindle rotates disk. Moving parts cause issues if dropped.

Magnetic platter stores data. Affected by heat and magnetic fields.

Iron particles on the disk are magnetised to be either north or south, representing 0 or 1.

Solid state disks (SSD)

SSDs look like a standard circuit board.
They use electrical circuits to persistently store data. These use microscopic transistors to control the flow of current. One that allows current to flow is a 1. Where current is blocked, a 0 is represented.

Optical drives (CD / Blu-Ray)

An optical drive uses a laser to reflect light off the surface of the disk. One long spiral track contains pits and lands. When the laser beam hits the curved start or end of a pit, the light is refracted and a 1 is recorded. Where light is reflected back directly from the flat bottom of a **pit**, or from an area of the track with no pit (a **land**) a 0 is recorded.

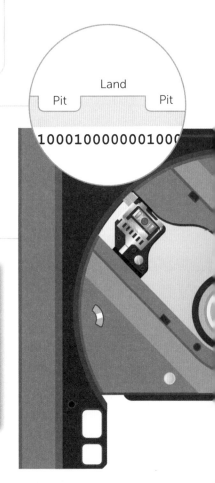

Land

Pit   Pit

1000100000001000

Explain why hard disk drives have been largely replaced by solid state drives in portable devices. [4]

Hard disk drives have lots of moving parts[1] which can cause problems if dropped or shaken[1]. The read/write head moves across the disk and can scratch the disk irreparably if accidentally moved too violently whilst in operation.[1] Moving the head across the disk to read or write data reduces the access speed[1] that can be achieved with solid state devices that have no moving parts. The cost and capacity of solid-state storage is improving.[1]

CLOUD STORAGE

Cloud storage refers to remote file storage on someone else's server. Often this is with a major third-party company such as Google, Microsoft or Dropbox.

Advantages compared to local storage	Disadvantages compared to local storage
No need to purchase local storage devices or employ maintenance staff. Online storage capacity can shrink or grow as you need it.	May need to commit to an annual subscription.
Files are automatically backed up on the Cloud. Cloud services may be used to backup local files.	Backup and restore may be slower than local storage depending on your Internet connection speed.
Greater fault tolerance than local storage.	Security of the data will be managed by a third party - outside of the user's control.
Remote access to files from any Internet connected device, anywhere in the world.	Need an Internet connection to access online data.
Enables file sharing and collaboration.	Limited or delayed support from the Cloud host.
One cloud storage centre is more environmentally friendly than millions of individual servers.	You may be responsible for any security breaches over the data, even though you had no direct control over its security.

Cloud storage has become increasingly popular with individuals.

Explain the reasons for the significant growth in usage over the past few years. [4]

Smartphone screen size has increased significantly, and these devices are able to display files.[1] The 4G and 5G networks have enabled much faster browsing[1] / download speeds to access online data[1]. Network security has improved[1] so users are becoming more comfortable with the risks associated with unauthorised access to their data.[1] Browser software and mobile applications have improved to display files with greater ease and accuracy[1]. Data centre availability and large capacity data storage costs have improved[1] enabling Cloud service providers to make their businesses commercially viable[1].

EMBEDDED SYSTEMS

An **embedded system** is used to control the function of electronic devices such as those commonly found in the home. They often don't need a full operating system since they perform limited and very specific tasks with their input frequently controlled by a button press or switch.

Embedded systems must be reliable since they cannot be modified once manufactured. The program that controls them is held in **Read Only Memory** (**ROM**). Assembly language is often used to develop software for embedded systems.

Examples of embedded systems include air conditioning or heating systems, radio alarm clocks, washing machines, fridges, microwave ovens and digital cameras.

Non-embedded systems are general purpose systems. Their software is usually installed on an SSD or HDD. They can be used for a variety of tasks. Examples include PCs, smartphones, tablets and Raspberry Pi computers.

Remember to give full answers to the questions – don't just list key words.

Jonny says that his car's satnav is an embedded system. State whether he is correct and explain your answer. [3]

Yes, he is correct.[1] It has one dedicated function[1] with simple controls. The user cannot change the software held in ROM within the embedded system.[1] The user cannot run other general software on it.[1]

EXAMINATION PRACTICE

1. A motorbike has two tyres, front (F) and rear (R). If the ignition (I) is on, and either one of the tyres is below the minimum air pressure, a warning light (W) is displayed.

   (a) Draw a logic circuit diagram for this scenario. [2]

   (b) Complete the truth table for this scenario. [4]

Front tyre pressure low (F)	Rear tyre pressure low (R)	Ignition on (I)	Working space (F or R)	Warning light on (W)
0	0	0		
0	0	1		

2. (a) Write a logic statement that describes the following logic circuit. [3]

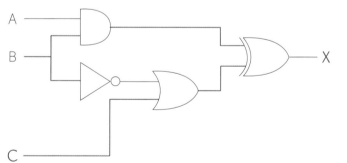

   (b) What will be the value of the output X if inputs A, B and C are all equal to 1? [1]

3. The operating system is responsible for processor management and security management.

   (a) Describe **one** task performed by the operating system to help maintain the security of a computer system. [2]

   (b) List **three** other functions of the operating system apart from processor management and security management. [3]

4. Which **one** of the following is an example of utility software? [1]
   A. Payroll software
   B. Compression software
   C. A mobile game app
   D. A word processor

5. Which **one** of the following best explains why an embedded system cannot be modified once manufactured? [1]
   A. The system uses secondary storage
   B. The casing is sealed
   C. The code is written in a low-level language
   D. The programs are stored in ROM

6. Shona is using a high-level language to learn programming. Describe **two** differences between a high-level language and a low-level language. [4]

7. Explain the difference between a compiler and an interpreter. [4]

8. Two components within a modern CPU are the Control Unit (CU) and the Arithmetic Logic Unit (ALU).
   Describe the function of each.
   (a) Control Unit [2]
   (b) Arithmetic Logic Unit [2]

9. Lindy has a new computer with 6 MB cache memory and 8 GB of RAM.
   (a) Explain how the use of cache memory can increase a computer's processing speed. [2]
   (b) State **one** reason why computers have less cache memory than random access memory. [1]

10. Two CPUs run at the same clock speed but one appears to be faster than the other.
    Explain how this might be possible. [4]

11. State **one** use of a ROM (Read-Only Memory) chip. [1]

12. A tablet computer is being designed with 256 GB storage.
    Suggest **one** suitable storage device. Justify your answer. [3]

13. ArcAccounts is a small accountancy firm. They are considering whether to move all their data from their own server to a Cloud-based service provider.
    Discuss the considerations the company should make before a decision is made. [6]

14. Describe the operation of a hard disk drive. [4]

NETWORKS

A **network** is defined as several computers connected together. A **stand-alone** computer has no connection to any other computer.

There are three main types of network: a **LAN** (**Local Area Network**), a **WAN** (**Wide Area Network**) and a **PAN** (**Personal Area Network**). A WAN connects LANs together to form larger networks.

The advantages of networking

Sharing resources

- Folders and files can be stored on a file server so they can be accessed by authorised users from any computer on the network.
- Peripheral devices such as printers and scanners can be shared.
- Internet connection can be shared.

Centralised management

- User profiles and security can all be managed centrally.
- Software can be distributed across the network rather than having to install it on each individual computer.
- All files can be backed up on a central server.

LAN

Operates on a single site or within a single organisation across buildings in a relatively small geographical area.

Uses Ethernet hardware and cabling that is usually owned and managed by the individual or organisation.

Examples include small company, school and home networks.

WAN

Used to transmit data over large distances, often nationally or internationally.

Uses third party or external hardware and cabling, including satellites, phone lines and the Internet.

Examples include the multi-national banking network and the Internet.

PAN

Used within a very limited area - usually within 10m.

Uses Bluetooth connections.

Examples include in-car handsfree systems and headphones.

Describe **two** disadvantages of networking computers. [4]

If the file server is switched off or the connection to it is damaged[1], your files and folders cannot be accessed.[1] Faults may cause a loss of data.[1] Networks require constant administration and management to keep them running smoothly,[1] and the larger the network becomes, the more difficult it is to manage. This can require expensive maintenance and a skilled workforce.[1]

Other points which would score marks include: Performance may degrade as traffic increases.[1] Viruses can spread from one computer to another.[1] Additional security will be required to prevent hackers from accessing data.[1]

WIRED AND WIRELESS NETWORKS

Data may be transmitted across a network using a **wired** or **wireless** connection.

Wired transmission media

Network cabling may be either **copper Ethernet cable**, which transmits data with electrical signals, or **fibre optic cable** which transmits data as pulses of light.

Ethernet cable is commonly used in small LANs. It is vulnerable to electromagnetic interference and data being transmitted is vulnerable to being intercepted by hackers. Fibre optic cable offers higher bandwidth, allowing larger amounts of data to be transferred simultaneously, and is often used for extremely high-speed data transfer over long distances. It is more expensive than copper cable.

Wireless transmission media

Wi-Fi uses radio waves to transmit data. As long as a device has a Wireless **NIC**, it can connect to a wireless network. Like Ethernet, Wi-Fi has its own set of rules to manage data transmission.

Bluetooth® is a radio-wave technology commonly used to connect devices within 10 metres of each other. Common uses include hands-free phone kits and smart speakers.

	Wired	Wireless
Transmission speed	Fast and consistent transmission speed	Typically slower than cabled connections
Expansion of network	Costly to add extra devices as additional cabling and switches may be required	Easy to connect additional devices, for example mobile and IoT devices, but additional devices will share the available bandwidth and increase the traffic
Interference	Copper cable can be susceptible to electrical or magnetic interference. Fibre optic cable avoids this	Wireless signals can be reduced by walls and interference from other wireless devices. This affects the connection speed
Signal strength	Ethernet cable maintains a good strength up to 100m, fibre optic cable can be much longer	Wireless hotspots are limited to a very small local area and require repeater devices to expand the range
Security	Data sent along cables cannot be easily intercepted	Wi Fi signals may be easily intercepted without adequate encryption security

Tick **one** box in each row of the table below to identify the most appropriate connection type for the given scenarios. [3]

Scenario	Wi-Fi	Ethernet
A customer seating area in a fast food restaurant	✓[1] *(portable devices)*	
A server connected to a school network		✓[1] *(high bandwidth)*
An old brick office building with very thick walls		✓[1] *(interference)*

TOPOLOGIES

There are two main networking structures or topologies covered in this course. These are **star** and **bus** topologies.

Star network

Star networks are most commonly used in businesses and organisations where performance and security are essential. They are also found in smaller offices and home networks owing to their simplicity. Each device on the network is connected to a **central switch** which routes transmissions to the correct device using its unique **MAC address**. A **router** can also operate as a switch.

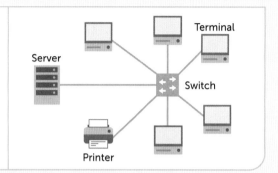

Give **two** advantages and **two** disadvantages of the star topology. [4]

Advantages: Very reliable as if one cable fails, the other nodes will be unaffected.[1] Data traffic on each cable is limited to that from one computer, significantly reducing data collisions.[1] Having fewer data collisions means consistently high network performance.[1]

Disadvantages: Expensive to install as it uses a lot of cable and requires a switch to direct transmission to the correct networked device.[1] If the switch fails, all devices on the network will lose their network connection.[1]

Bus network

Bus networks can be used to connect computers in a small organisation. All signals are transmitted through a single backbone cable (or bus). There are terminators fitted to either end to prevent stray signals bouncing back down the cable.

Advantages
- Simple to install.
- A single cable significantly reduces cabling costs.

Disadvantages
- A cable failure in the main bus will affect the entire network.
- Performance of the network degrades quickly with more users. The data packets collide with each other as they travel in both directions on the same cable, and have to be retransmitted.
- Each computer attached to the cable can 'see' all data travelling up and down it which can be a security risk.

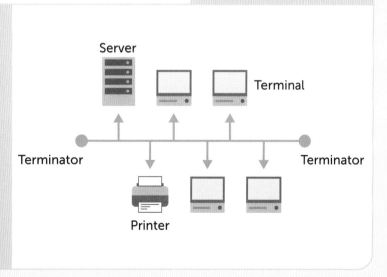

NETWORK PROTOCOLS

Data transmission and communications standards have been developed to ensure that all connected devices can communicate seamlessly with each other using the same set of rules. A **protocol** is a set of **rules**. A network protocol defines the standards for data transmission.

The Highway Code establishes the rules for drivers in the UK. Without a standard, traffic would crash far more often. Likewise, English is a standard protocol for communication in the UK. Without a common language, communication would be very difficult. Imagine giving driving directions while blindfolded to someone using another language!

Ethernet and Wi-Fi

Ethernet refers to a set of related protocols or rules commonly used across Local Area Networks to govern how data is sent and received. **Wi-Fi** (Wireless LAN) is another family of related protocols which uses radio waves to transmit data. As long as a device has a Wireless **Network Interface Card** (**NIC**), it can connect to a wireless network. Like Ethernet, Wi-Fi has its own set of rules to manage data transmission.

Different protocols are used for different purposes:

Protocol	Purpose	Key features
HTTP (Hypertext Transfer Protocol)	Used by a browser to access a webpage from a web server	Delivers web page data
HTTPS (Hypertext Transfer Protocol Secure)	As HTTP with encryption	Encrypts the data and uses a secure socket layer for greater protection
FTP (File Transfer Protocol)	Transmitting files between client and server computers	Used to upload and download files from a server
UDP (User Datagram Protocol)	An alternative to **TCP** (see next page)	Commonly used for online gaming and DNS
IMAP (Internet Message Access Protocol)	Accessing email on a mail server via multiple devices	Maintains synchronisation of an email account across all devices
SMTP (Simple Mail Transfer Protocol)	Sending email messages between mail servers	Used for sending only

Bilal accesses his bank via an online banking website on his tablet computer.

Once logged in, Bilal can access his account data.

(a) Give a suitable protocol that could be used to transmit his account data. [1]

(b) Give **one** reason for your choice of protocol. [1]

(c) Bilal's bank sends him regular emails. Explain **two** protocols that are used in the sending and retrieval of email. [4]

(a) HTTPS[1], (b) HTTPS is a secure protocol that encrypts data in transmission.[1] (c) SMTP[1] is used to send the email to the bank's mail server.[1] This is passed to the client mail server.[1] POP or IMAP[1] is used to retrieve the email by Bilal's email client.[1]

TCP/IP LAYERS

Transmission Control Protocol / Internet Protocol (TCP/IP) is a set of protocols operating on different layers. A **layer** provides a division of network functionality so that each layer can operate and be updated completely independently of any other layer.

The 4-layer TCP/IP model

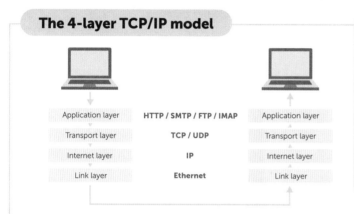

Application layer	HTTP / SMTP / FTP / IMAP	Application layer
Transport layer	TCP / UDP	Transport layer
Internet layer	IP	Internet layer
Link layer	Ethernet	Link layer

An IP address is a unique public address for the router or gateway of a network. Data packets use this address to travel to the router, after which point they are directed using an internal (private) IP address within the network. Private addresses are not unique and the IP address of a portable device such as a laptop will change when it is moved, for example between towns.

The roles of each layer

The **application layer** selects the most appropriate **protocol** based on the application operating on that layer. For example, HTTP or HTTPS would be used if using a browser, or SMTP for email.

The **transport layer** establishes a connection with the recipient computer. It then splits the data into manageable chunks called **packets** and gives them a packet number, (e.g. Packet 1 of 40) before they are passed on to the Internet Layer. Any lost packets are resent. The transport layer also reassembles any packets received into the right order.

The **Internet layer** packages or unpackages data, adds the destination **IP address** and routes the packet to the next router on the way to its destination. Routers operate on the Internet layer.

The **link layer** is the physical hardware connection between network nodes. It uses the **MAC address** of Network Interface Cards to identify specific devices.

Describe **two** benefits of using protocol layers.   [4]

Layers are self-contained with their own separate purposes[1] so manufacturers of hardware and software that operate on one layer need only be concerned with that layer's protocols[1]. This makes it possible for hardware from one manufacturer designed specifically to work on one particular layer to work with hardware produced for another layer by another manufacturer.[1] Software developers are also able to edit one layer without affecting others.[1] Layers provide more manageable divisions of work than one larger system.[1]

NETWORK SECURITY

Networks require security measures to prevent unauthorised access. This ensures the privacy of data that is transferred within the network. Using a combination of methods provides greater protection against threats.

Authentication

Authentication of an individual is used to make sure that a person is who they say they are.

Most commonly, this is done by asking a user to enter their **ID and password** or **PIN**. This is then authenticated by comparing it with the saved password previously stored on a database. A simple authentication routine is used when you log into a school network, or an online shopping site.

Email confirmation is frequently used to confirm that a user has access to the email address they may have used to register with a website. An email with an activation link or code is sent to the email address that users can click to confirm they have access to the email inbox. They can then complete the registration process.

Biometric methods of authentication include optical, facial or fingerprint recognition. These use a person's physical features to confirm their identity.

Firewall

A firewall is a software or hardware device that monitors all incoming and outgoing network traffic. Using a set of rules, it decides whether to block or allow specific data packets. By opening and closing ports, it can block traffic from disallowed connections from accessing the network, as well as blocking outgoing communications from the network, to make sure that only authorised traffic is permitted.

MAC address filtering

A **Media Access Control (MAC) address** is a **unique hexadecimal identification number** assigned to every **Network Interface Card** used in networked devices.

MAC address: 30-A5-BD-6F-C4-63

A router can prevent devices from connecting to it based on their MAC address. This will prevent those computers from accessing the network. This is known as **MAC address filtering**.

Explain how MAC address filtering is used to restrict access to a network. [2]

The address of each device attempting to connect to a network is looked up in a predetermined list of addresses allowed or denied by the router[1]. The router then makes a decision as to whether the network can be accessed.[1]

ENCRYPTION

Encryption is the process of encoding data so that it cannot be easily understood if it is discovered, stolen or intercepted.

An unencrypted message or dataset is known as **plaintext**. This is converted into **ciphertext** by encoding it using a mathematical encryption algorithm and key. Both the key and the algorithm are required to encode or decode data.

Simple encryption with a pre-shared key works like this:

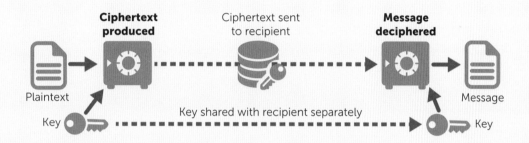

Caesar Cipher

A very primitive encryption algorithm was said to be invented by Julius Caesar. This is known as the Caesar cipher. This is a substitution cipher where each letter is replaced by another. The key in this instance would be 3 as A translates to D, three letters along the alphabet.

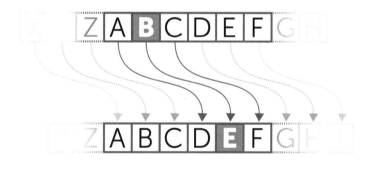

Jonny says that he has encrypted his work so that no one else can access it.

Explain why this isn't strictly true. [2]

Encryption encodes data making it unintelligible[1], but it could still be read, even if it would not make any sense to anyone who did not have the decryption key[1].

Using the same principle, decode the message "LSPH JMVI" using a key of 4.

EXAMINATION PRACTICE

1. Moshin is planning to network several computers in a small office using a star topology.
   (a) State **three** advantages of linking computers in a LAN. [3]
   (b) Draw a diagram of the star topology. [3]
   (c) State **one** type of cable that Moshin could use for the star network. [1]
   (d) Describe **one** method of authentication that Moshin could use to restrict access to the network to authorised users only. [3]

   Moshin wants to connect his tablet to the network wirelessly. A wireless connection requires additional security to ensure that data transmissions sent by one device cannot be understood if they are intercepted before they reach the recipient device.
   (e) State the name of this security method. [1]
   (f) Explain how this process works. [2]

2. Explain **two** differences between a Local Area Network and a Wide Area Network. [4]

3. A travel speaker has been designed to use Bluetooth technology to connect to a nearby mobile phone.
   (a) State the name of this type of network. [1]
   (b) Explain why Bluetooth is a more appropriate connection than a wired or Wi-Fi connection for the speaker. [3]

4. Abi enters the URL www.bbc.co.uk into her browser. A protocol is a common set of rules used by Abi's browser to download the web page from the web server.
   (a) State which protocol the web browser will use to download the web page information from the web server. [1]
   (b) Explain why a standard protocol is necessary. [2]

   Web traffic is passed up and down layers in the TCP/IP protocol stack.
   (c) (i) State which layer Abi's browser would operate on. [1]
       (ii) Explain the purpose of the Transport layer. [3]

5. Four possible methods used for protecting data on a network are shown on the left.
   Draw lines to match each description of an issue to the most appropriate protection method. [4]

Issue
Internal hacker illegally accessing files and changing or deleting data on a LAN
Hackers attempting to access ports on a server which are not in use
Users attempting to connect to a Wi-Fi access point they are disallowed from using
Confidential data transmitted over the Internet being read

Protection method
Firewall
Encryption
MAC address filtering
User authentication

CYBER SECURITY THREATS

Cyber security relates to the processes, policies and practices designed to protect against any threats or unauthorised access to networks, computers, programs or data. A combination of strategies should be employed to provide a robust defence against these threats.

Threats

Access rights

Misconfigured access rights allow some employees too much access to data. This could become an issue if the employee abuses this or if their account is compromised. Different **user access levels** can be granted to each employee of an organisation based on their needs. This limits the amount of data that a hacker is able to see if an account is compromised. Few employees will have access to everything.

Passwords

Weak passwords consisting of fewer than eight characters, which include no special characters, taking the form of whole words or dates are easily guessed. Strong passwords should include numbers, upper- and lower-case letters and special characters, e.g. $, %, >. Passwords should never be written down and should be regularly changed. Default passwords should always be changed.

Pharming

Pharming is a type of cyber-attack; cybercriminals install malicious code on your computer designed to redirect website traffic intended for one site, to a fake, official-looking website. This can be used to harvest personal details from unsuspecting visitors. It is prevented by using an up-to-date virus checker.

Removable media

Removable media, such as USB flash drives, should be regularly scanned for viruses each time they are transferred between computers. Some companies disallow their use as they are a significant way of spreading malware.

Software

Unpatched or **outdated software** can leave an organisation open to new threats designed to take advantage of known weaknesses in systems. Patches and upgrades can be downloaded from software manufacturers to improve security and fix holes.

1. Explain **one** reason why you should never use a USB flash drive without knowing its origin. [2]
2. Explain what is meant by "user access levels" in a school computer system. [2]

1. *Some removeable storage devices are deliberately infected[1] and left where they may be picked up and used by someone.[1] This is known as 'baiting'.*
2. *Staff in different departments will only have access to parts of the system which they need for their jobs.[1] E.g. Teachers will not be able to access payroll or personnel data, and students will not have access to teaching administration or exam data. Senior management will have a high access level and be able to access many more parts of the system.[1]*

PENETRATION TESTING

Penetration testing

Penetration testing, or **pen testing**, is used to find weaknesses in a system by employing someone to break in. These vulnerabilities can then be fixed before a hacker has an opportunity to discover and exploit them.

Black-box pen testing

Black-box pen testing (**External pen testing**) aims to discover flaws and back doors into a system from outside the organisation – this might target servers and firewalls. This is done without the knowledge or use of usernames, passwords or access codes.

White-box pen testing

White-box pen testing (**Internal pen testing**) puts the tester in the position of an employee or malicious insider who may already have a degree of access into the system. Just how much damage could a dishonest employee cause?

Explain **one** advantage of white-box penetration testing over black-box testing. [2]

White box testing allows access with full transparency of the ways in which an organisation works, its infrastructure and its code.[1] This extends the testing area beyond where black-box testing can reach. This can find issues arising from a well-informed, 'inside job' by a disgruntled employee.[1]

SOCIAL ENGINEERING

Social engineering uses manipulation to dishonestly persuade someone to divulge personal information by deception.

Phishing

Phishing emails redirect a user to a fake website where they trick the reader into divulging confidential information such as passwords that can be used fraudulently. Email and SMS messages are commonly used for this with fake offers of prize draw 'wins'.

Shouldering

Shouldering or **shoulder surfing** means to look over someone's shoulder when they enter a password or PIN.

Blagging

Blagging is the art of creating a fake scenario in which a victim may feel it is appropriate to divulge information they would not give out under ordinary circumstances.

Suggest **one** method to reduce the risks of shouldering when entering a PIN into an electronic Chip and PIN machine. [2]

Cover your hand when entering your PIN.[1] Ensure that nobody is directly behind you or within line of sight of your hand.[1] Stand close to the machine to obscure others' view.[1]

MALICIOUS CODE (MALWARE)

Malware describes malicious software written to cause inconvenience or damage to programs or data.

Virus

A **virus** is a program that is installed on a computer without the user's knowledge or permission with the purpose of doing harm. It includes instructions to replicate (copy itself) automatically on a computer and to other computers.

Trojan

A **Trojan**, named after the famous Ancient Greek story of the Trojan Horse, is a program which masquerades as having one legitimate purpose but actually has another. It is normally spread by email. The user is invited to click on a link for some everyday or interesting purpose, which then executes a program which may, for example, give the controller unauthorised access to that computer.

Spyware

Spyware is software that gathers information about a person or organisation without their knowledge. It is often used to track and store a users' movements on the Internet. Some spyware may change computer settings, making unauthorised changes to browser settings or changes to software settings. It can also be used to collect personal information such as user logins or bank details.

Discuss methods that could be used to prevent or minimise the impact of malware infections on a company network.

[6]

Anti-malware software should be current and set to automatically screen new files[1] and regularly scan the hard disk or server.[1] Macro scripts in files should be blocked[1] as these commonly contain malicious code[1]. Regular backups will ensure that data can be restored if lost or damaged.[1] Backups should be regularly tested, stored off-site, and on a disk separate from the main network[1] so they are not affected by the same conditions as the current data[1]. Email links and attachments should be blocked or disabled.[1] Emails from unknown parties should not be opened.[1] Staff should be appropriately trained to recognise threats and the strategies to prevent them.[1] Pop-ups should be disabled using a pop-up blocker and the correct browser settings.[1] Software should not be downloaded unless authorised by a network administrator.[1] It should be up-to-date with the most recent patches.[1] A firewall or filter can be used to block access to certain devices or websites.[1] Employees should not be allowed to bring in removable media or use them on company computers.[1] Refer to the band descriptions for extended response questions on Page 101.

METHODS TO DETECT AND PREVENT CYBER SECURITY THREATS

Biometrics

Biometrics use pre-recorded human characteristics to authenticate authorised users of a system or device.

Methods include:
- Facial recognition
- Iris and retina scanners
- Fingerprint or palm recognition
- Voice recognition

The user is required to look at a camera, press their fingerprint to a sensor or speak into a microphone. The image or recording is taken and analysed for key features. This is compared with several pre-recorded examples for that individual and if a match is found, access is granted.

Email authentication

Email authentication is used to send a code or link to an email address provided by a user. If they click on the link in the email, it authenticates them as the user of that email account.

Passwords

Password systems are effective at reducing access to systems. Passwords should be secure and changed regularly.

Automatic software updates

Automatic software updates will keep applications and the operating system constantly up-to-date. This enables bugs and security flaws in the software to be fixed as soon as they are known about with a **patch**.

CAPTCHA

CAPTCHA stands for Completely Automated Public Turing test to tell Computers and Humans Apart. It provides obscured words which computers are unable to recognise or detect. This prevents bots from successfully masquerading as humans.

Type the two words:

CAPTCHA
Privacy - Terms

Amber stores confidential information on the tablet computer that she uses for her job.

(a) Give **two** ways in which Amber could restrict unauthorised access to her data. [2]

(b) Describe the problems that could result if Amber's tablet is hacked. [3]

(a) Amber could use two-factor authentication by sending a code to her mobile phone which has to be typed on the tablet to gain access[1], use biometrics such as face or fingerprint recognition to log in[1], limit the attempts allowed to log in before being locked out[1], create a strong PIN or password[1], avoid leaving the tablet unattended / keep it locked in a drawer overnight so that others cannot physically access it[1], or avoid connecting to unsecured Wi-Fi networks[1].

(b) Amber's data may be stolen[1] and passed on to criminal third parties[1]. This may break the Data Protection Act 2018 regarding appropriate security[1], her employment may be affected[1], her files may be changed or deleted[1], or she may be locked out of her own tablet[1]. Data may be leaked to the public or newspapers[1], or the organisation she works for could be held to ransom[1].

EXAMINATION PRACTICE

1. A bank holds data on a database kept on the organisation's server about each of its account holders, including personal data, credit rating, credit limit and current balance.

   Social engineering techniques have been used by callers contacting their call centre.

   (a) Explain what is meant by social engineering. [2]

   (b) Give **one** possible consequence of such an attack on each of:

   (i) The bank's customers [1]

   (ii) The bank's staff [1]

2. Sylvia runs a small accounting business from home. She keeps details of all her customers on her desktop computer.

   Describe **two** ways in which this data may be put at risk and suggest a way of reducing the risk in each case. [4]

3. A network manager is carrying out a penetration test.

   (a) Explain the purpose of penetration testing. [2]

   (b) Describe the principles of how an internal ("white box") penetration test is carried out. [3]

4. Roshin has received an email from an unrecognised sender.

   (a) Give **three** ways in which a phishing attack by email may be recognised. [3]

   (b) Describe **one** possible consequence of a phishing attack. [2]

5. Five cyber security terms are given below. For each row in the table below, choose the letter A, B, C, D or E that best matches the description. Letters should not be used more than once. [3]

   A. Pharming

   B. Trojan

   C. Virus

   D. Biometrics

   E. CAPTCHA

Description	Letter
Malware that automatically replicates itself on a computer.	
A cyber-attack designed to redirect legitimate website traffic to a fake website.	
Use of human features for authentication.	

DATABASE CONCEPTS

A **database** is a way of holding data in an organised way so that searching for data items that meet certain criteria is quick and easy.

Tables, records and fields

A database consists of one or more **tables**. Each table consists of many **records** (rows) each having an identical record structure. Each **field** (column) in a record has a defined field type such as integer, real, date, currency, Boolean or string.

Each table will have a **primary key** field that uniquely identifies each record in the table. In this table, the primary key is **ID**.

VolcanoTable

ID	name	country	lastErupted	explosivityIndex	elevationMetres
1	Taal	Philippines	2020	4	311
2	White Island	New Zealand	2019	2	321
3	Shiveluch	Russia	2019	4	3283
4	Anak Krakatoa	Indonesia	2018	3	813
5	Eyjafjallajökull	Iceland	2010	4	2119
6	Etna	Italy	2013	3	3350
7	Stromboli	Italy	2019	2	924
8	Puyehue-Cordón Caulle	Chile	2011	5	2236

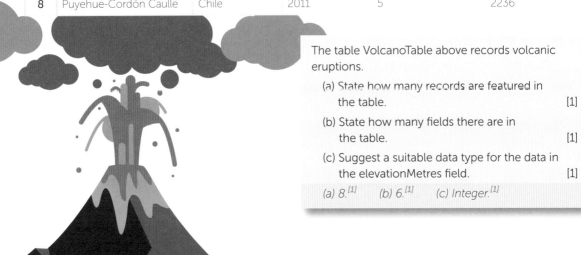

The table VolcanoTable above records volcanic eruptions.

(a) State how many records are featured in the table. [1]

(b) State how many fields there are in the table. [1]

(c) Suggest a suitable data type for the data in the elevationMetres field. [1]

(a) 8.[1]   (b) 6.[1]   (c) Integer.[1]

STRUCTURED QUERY LANGUAGE (SQL)

Records in a database format can be searched using a Structured Query Language (SQL).

The format of an SQL statement

SELECT... list the field(s) you want displayed here
FROM... list the table or tables the data will come from here
WHERE... list search criteria here
ORDER BY... optional criteria to sort in ascending (ASC) or descending (DESC) order.

Using the Volcano table opposite, the SQL statement below will return a results table showing all eruptions since 2019, in ascending alphabetical order of name.

    SELECT name, lastErupted, explosivityIndex
    FROM VolcanoTable
    WHERE lastErupted >= 2019
    ORDER BY name ASC

Wildcards

The wildcard * is a substitute for ALL fields, e.g. SELECT *
The Boolean condition LIKE is used with the wildcard %, which is a substitute for zero or more characters, e.g.
    WHERE name **LIKE** 'S%'
finds all records with names beginning with S.

Results table

name	lastErupted	explosivityIndex
Shiveluch	2019	4
Stromboli	2019	2
Taal	2020	4
White Island	2019	2

You can also use Boolean operators to search for data. To find the volcanoes which either have an explosivityIndex of 5, or have an elevation below 500 metres:

    SELECT name, country, lastErupted, elevationMetres
    FROM VolcanoTable
    WHERE explosivityIndex = 5 OR elevationMetres < 500
    ORDER BY lastErupted DESC

Results table

name	country	lastErupted	elevationMetres
Taal	Philippines	2020	311
White Island	New Zealand	2019	321
Puyehue-Cordón Caulle	Chile	2011	2236

RELATIONAL DATABASES

A **relational database** consists of two or more tables, connected to each other through the use of a common field.

Each table will have a **primary key** field that uniquely identifies each record in the table.

Example

In the Mission table below, the primary key is **missionID**.

Mission

missionID	commander	launchDate	days	moonLanding	landingSite
Apollo 10	Thomas Stafford, Air Force	18/05/1969	8	No	No landing
Apollo 11	Neil Armstrong, Civilian	16/07/1969	5	Yes	Mare Tranquilitatis
Apollo 12	Charles Conrad, Navy	14/11/1969	5	Yes	Ocean of Storms
Apollo 13	Jim Lovell, Navy	11/04/1970	6	No	Aborted
Apollo 14	Alan Shepard, Navy	31/01/1971	6	Yes	Littrow crater
Apollo 15	David Scott, Air Force	02/08/1971	12	Yes	Censorinus crater
Apollo 16	John Young, Navy	16/04/1972	11	Yes	Descartes Highlands
Apollo 17	Gene Cernan, Navy	07/12/1972	12	Yes	Marius Hills
Skylab 2	Thomas Stafford, Air Force	25/05/1973	28	No	No landing

Relationships

A mission can have only one commander, but a commander can fly on many missions. This one-to-many relationship can be represented using an entity relationship diagram:

Commander $\quad$ 1 $\qquad$ ∞ $\quad$ Mission

Other possible examples of relationships are many-to-one, one-to-one and many-to-many:

Person $\quad$ 1 $\qquad$ 1 $\quad$ Passport

Author $\quad$ ∞ $\qquad$ ∞ $\quad$ Book

Data inconsistency and data redundancy

The data in this database contains **repeating fields** or **redundant data**. Some astronaut commanders (Thomas Stafford) feature more than once in the table and therefore their details are unnecessarily repeated. This repeated data is redundant data. The individual instances of this repeating data could also result in **inconsistency** over time by updating different records with conflicting data for the same person, for example.

A further problem with this table is that the name held in the commander field is not in a format that can be easily searched. It actually holds three pieces of information. Each field in a database should be **atomic**, holding only one piece of data, e.g. surname, firstname, military service.

To avoid data redundancy and inconsistency, each data item should be held just once. This involves splitting the table into two – one for each **entity** or thing. In this case, the two entities are mission and commander. A link, or relationship, is then created between them both.

The new tables would look like this. The primary key from the Commander table (commanderID) is also used in the Mission table. In the Mission table it is referred to as a **foreign key**.

Mission

missionID	commanderID	launchDate	days	moonLanding	landingSite
Apollo 10	1001	18/05/1969	8	No	No landing
Apollo 11	1002	16/07/1969	5	Yes	Mare Tranquilitatis
Apollo 12	1003	14/11/1969	5	Yes	Ocean of Storms
Apollo 13	1004	11/04/1970	6	No	Aborted
Apollo 14	1005	31/01/1971	6	Yes	Littrow crater
Apollo 15	1006	02/08/1971	12	Yes	Censorinus crater
Apollo 16	1007	16/04/1972	11	Yes	Descartes Highlands
Apollo 17	1008	07/12/1972	12	Yes	Marius Hills
Skylab 2	1001	25/05/1973	28	No	No landing

1. The table **Mission** records Apollo moon missions.

   (a) Suggest a suitable data type for the data in the moonLanding field. [1]

   (b) Explain why missionID is the only suitable field for the primary key. [2]

   (a) Boolean.[1] (b) missionID is the only field which contains data that will always be unique.[1] It would be possible for all data in other fields to be repeated[1] in other missions to the same sites, on the same days or using the same astronauts.

Commander

commanderID	firstname	surname	militaryService
1001	Thomas	Stafford	Air Force
1002	Neil	Armstrong	Civilian
1003	Charles	Conrad	Navy
1004	Jim	Lovell	Navy
1005	Alan	Shepard	Navy
1006	David	Scott	Air Force
1007	John	Young	Navy
1008	Gene	Cernan	Navy

2. Suggest a suitable relationship type for two entities car and maker. [1]

   Many to one.[1]

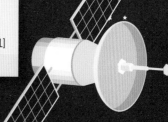

USING SQL TO RETRIEVE DATA FROM TWO TABLES

The database about Apollo moon missions consists of two tables. Data from more than one table can be retrieved in a single search using an additional criterion in the WHERE clause to match the primary key of one table against the foreign key in another.

Example

To display the missionID, launchDate, firstname and surname of the commanders of all the missions that took place in 1969:

SELECT missionID, launchDate, firstname, surname
FROM Mission, Commander
WHERE (launchDate **BETWEEN** #01/01/1969# **AND** #31/12/1969#)
    AND (Mission.commanderID = Commander.commanderID)
ORDER BY launchdate **ASC**

Results table

missionID	launchDate	firstname	surname
Apollo 10	18/05/1969	Thomas	Stafford
Apollo 11	16/07/1969	Neil	Armstrong
Apollo 12	14/11/1969	Charles	Conrad

1. Use the data in the tables on the previous page for this question.

Complete the table below to show the results from the following query:

SELECT missionID, firstname, surname, launchDate, landingSite
FROM Mission, Commander
WHERE (moonLanding = No) **AND** (launchDate >= #01/01/1970#)
    AND (Mission.commanderD = Commander.commanderD)
ORDER BY launchDate **DESC**   [4]

missionID	firstName	surname	launchDate	landingSite	
Skylab2	Thomas	Stafford	25/05/1973	No landing	[2]
Apollo 13	Jim	Lovell	11/04/1970	Aborted	[2]

USING SQL TO EDIT DATABASE DATA

Using SQL to insert data into a database

The SQL **INSERT INTO** statement is used to insert a new record into a database table. The syntax is:

> **INSERT INTO** tableName (column1, column 2 ...)
> **VALUES** (value1, value2 ...)

Example

To add a new record to the Commander table:

> **INSERT INTO** Commander (commanderID, firstname)
> **VALUES** (1000, 'Unmanned')

Note that strings are entered in quotes. Some fields in this record will be left blank.

Using SQL to edit data in a database

The SQL **UPDATE** statement is used to amend a record in a database table. The syntax is as follows:

> **UPDATE** tableName
> **SET** column1 = value1, column2 = value2 ...
> **WHERE** condition

Example

To correct the launchDate for Apollo 15 to 26/07/1971:

> **UPDATE Mission**
> **SET launchDate = #26/07/1971#**
> **WHERE missionID = 'Apollo 15'**

Note that strings are entered in quotes. Some fields in this record will be left blank.

Using SQL to delete a record in a database

To delete a record from a table, the syntax is:

> **DELETE FROM** tableName
> **WHERE** Condition

2. Write SQL statements to:

(a) Insert into the Mission table, a new record for Explorer 49, an Unmanned spacecraft that was launched on 10 June 1973 and orbited the moon without landing. Explorer 49 was launched on 10 June 1973. An unmanned mission has the commanderID of 1000. [2]

(b) Edit the Military Service of Neil Armstrong, commanderID 1002, to 'Air Force'. [3]

(c) Delete the record for Apollo 13. [2]

(a) INSERT INTO Mission (missionID,commanderID, launchDate, moonLanding, landingSite)[1]
VALUES ('Explorer 49', 1000, #10/06/1973#, No, 'No landing')[1]

(b) UPDATE Commander[1]
SET militaryService = 'Air Force'[1]
WHERE commanderID = '1002'[1]

(c) DELETE FROM Mission[1]
WHERE missionID = 'Apollo 13'[1]

EXAMINATION PRACTICE

1. Five database terms are given below. For each row in the table, give **one** letter which best matches the description. [3]

A. Record   B. Field   C. Primary key   D. Foreign key   E. Relationship

Definition	Letter
A column of data	
Uniquely identifies a row of data in a database	
A link between two tables	

2. Two database tables are given below.

Holder

holderID	firstname	surname	nationality
WRH1034	Florence	Joyner	American
WRH1375	Sven	Ohler	German
WRH1008	Ashrita	Furman	American
WRH1916	Leah	Shutkever	British

Event

eventID	title	speed	year	holderID
1	Fastest burrito eaten	35.26s	2019	WRH1916
2	Fastest mobility scooter	180 kmh	2017	WRH1375
3	Fastest mile space hopper	13m 0s	2010	WRH1008
4	Fastest mile forward rolls	19m 11s	2000	WRH1008

(a) State how many records there are in the Event table. [1]

(b) From the tables above, give an example of a foreign key field. Your answer should be in the format **table.field**. [1]

(c) Explain how this relational database eliminates issues with data redundancy and inconsistency. [4]

(d) Write an SQL query to return the firstname, surname and nationality of all American world record holders in an event. Order the results in ascending order by surname. [4]

(e) (i) Write a query to display the surname, event title and speed of all world records beaten after 2015. Order the results in descending order of year. [4]

(ii) Complete the table below to show the results of the query. [2]

surname	title	speed

(f) State the purpose of the following SQL statement:

UPDATE Event
SET speed = '182.4 kmh'
WHERE eventID = 2 [2]

(g) Write a statement to delete Florence Joyner from the Holder table. [2]

ETHICAL, LEGAL AND ENVIRONMENTAL IMPACTS OF DIGITAL TECHNOLOGY ON WIDER SOCIETY

New technologies often introduce new issues. Exam questions on ethical, legal and environmental impacts will be taken from the following areas:

Cyber security and hacking

Hacking means unauthorised access to programs or data. The growing use of communications technologies has vastly increased the volume of sensitive data that is sent electronically. People need to be increasingly careful with the data they send, and think about how they can avoid cyber threats. Software and hardware can be put in place to prevent unauthorised access to a computer system (hacking).

Encryption is commonly used to secure data, but cyber criminals are also using the same security methods to protect their data from governments and law enforcement agencies. Should security services have access to everyone's encrypted data in order to protect the majority from the few?

Some governments argue that they should have access to all encrypted data sent to or from their citizens. Discuss how this might impact governments and citizens.   [4]

Governments would have greater control over the protection of their citizens[1] if they are able to analyse communications that may relate to planned criminal activity or acts of terrorism[1], for example. Citizens value their privacy[1] and may not like the fact that governments may be 'watching' or 'reading' their messages, emails and other communications.[1]

Mobile technologies

Mobile technologies such as smartphones and laptops switch from one network to another almost seamlessly as they roam through various regions. Any data sent through these networks needs to be secure. An unprotected network connection can allow a **hacker** to intercept any data, including passwords, online shopping data and bank details. **Phishing** scams are increasingly happening via SMS messaging instead of standard email.

Police have access to mobile phone cell data. This can effectively be used to track the movement of a phone. Like a breadcrumb trail, each time a phone makes contact with the nearest mobile mast it gives away its location. This data, and the communications to and from a device, are commonly used in crime prevention and as evidence in **legal** cases.

Wireless networking

Users of an unsecured connection should be very wary of what data they are sending. There may be **eavesdroppers** within the network looking to capitalise on sensitive data that may be sent.

K9Track is a new device designed to be attached to a dog collar. It allows the owner to track the pet's location on a connected smartphone and to monitor the animal's health and levels of exercise each day.

Discuss the ethical, legal and privacy issues that should be considered when creating tracking and monitoring technology such as K9Track.   [6]

Since a dog is commonly with their owner, such a tracking device will also be effectively tracking and recording the movements of the (various) owners.[1] The use of this data will need to be securely stored by the app or cloud service provider.[1]

The costs of pet insurance or veterinary bills may reduce if its health and movements are monitored and regularly checked.[1] This may benefit those who can afford the high cost of new devices[1], widening the digital divide between those who can and cannot afford technology[1].

The algorithms used to determine what levels of exercise are healthy and what are not for each individual pet will need to be very accurate[1], taking into prior account an animal's size, weight, breed and general health[1]. Inaccuracies could lead to blame if an animal's lack of exercise were the cause of ill health[1].

Monitoring and tracking your pet's movements provides another reason to check your smartphone[1], increasing the amount of (unnecessary) time spent using technology and looking at screens[1]. This may negatively impact or reduce the time spent with the pet or family.[1]

The security of the data[1] gathered, both accessible through the mobile app and in its raw form stored by the manufacturer will need to be carefully protected from unauthorised access[1]. A biometric access key[1] could be used to access the mobile phone app, and the stored data should be adequately protected[1] (under the Data Protection Act) from malware[1], hackers[1] (unauthorised access), social engineering[1] and interception[1].

Marks are indicative only. Refer to the band descriptions and levels of response guidance for extended response questions on page 101.

This essay style question is assessed against the levels of response guidelines on page 101. The quality of written communication, including spelling, punctuation and grammar may also be assessed through your response to similar questions.

Cloud storage

Cloud storage is the term used for remote storage, accessible via the Internet. Instead of every individual or company having their own storage devices with unused capacity, a cloud storage provider (e.g. Google, Dropbox) offers a cheaper and more environmentally friendly alternative. These huge storage locations, that thousands of users can access securely, are increasingly powered by renewable energy.

Other advantages include:

- Cloud storage can be accessed from anywhere in the world with an Internet connection.
- This enables thousands of people to work from home rather than travel to work, which means fewer polluting cars on the road.
- It makes it easier to share data with others.
- Backup is arranged by the cloud storage provider.

Disadvantages:

- Increased security risks as more data is shared over a connection.
- High bandwidth is required to access data and is not universally available.

Computer-based implants

Implanted technologies include microchips that are inserted under the skin, cochlear implants and pacemakers.

Recently, there have been discussions about whether thousands, or millions, of people should have microchips implanted for a range of applications, for example:

- Employees of a technology company in Wisconsin had a microchip injected in their hands for security convenience.
- Chips could bring health advantages: for example, monitor and alert a wearer to a current risk of a heart attack.
- A farm could track livestock movements.

But what are the wider issues involved?

Privacy and security issues:

- Who owns the data on the chip? Who has access to the data?
- Do chips communicate with outside networks?
- Can the chips be hacked and manipulated?

Legal issues:

- What laws are in place to define what is legal in implanting and using chips?

Ethical issues:

- What might be the good or evil outcomes? Will it always be voluntary to be "chipped"?
- Will ethical and moral processes and procedures be breached by hackers?
- Are chip implants forbidden by some religions?

Autonomous vehicles

Self-driving vehicles are becoming an increasingly common phenomenon globally. Like most new technologies, they come with several factors that should be carefully considered before introduction in society.

- **Ethical** issues arise such as how the car should be programmed to respond should an object, animal, child or group of adults, for example, suddenly appear in the road. Applying the brakes hard immediately shifts the risk from the obstacle to the passengers, but is this always the right decision? Eastern and western societies have differing views on who should be spared in such incidents if an accident is likely to harm at least one party inside or outside of the vehicle. Under normal circumstances, the driver is responsible for such decisions.

- **Legal** issues: In the event of an accident and ensuing legal cases, who takes the blame? The programmer, the manufacturer, the driver or someone else? What if the driver has a setting for a driving preference which increases risk for some while reducing it for others?

- **Privacy** concerns may arise where cars enable location tracking for navigation and security. Car ownership data may be able to authenticate authorised use of the vehicle for safety and insurance. Matching the two data sets, however, provides a very accurate view of who goes where, when, and with whom.

- **Environmental** issues in battery production and the generation of additional electric power required to run a nation of electric vehicles also needs careful consideration.

Driverless cars are currently being tested on public roads. Discuss the ethical and legal issues that should be considered when creating autonomous vehicles. [6]

Ethical issues include safer driving (and more lawful driving) as there is no room for human error or poor judgement regarding traffic regulations.[1] Some machines may not be sophisticated enough to make snap decisions that affect lives.[1] They can only react to facts and not feeling or emotion.[1] Journey tracking, driver identification and the use of this data[1] (as discussed opposite). Pollution may lessen given zero emissions in autonomous (commonly electric) cars[1], but it may increase in other areas of the electricity and production supply chains[1].

Legal issues include liability in the event of an accident[1], insurance requirements[1], cyber security of computerised vehicles[1] – vehicle theft may be possible through hacking[1]. The privacy of location and customer data would need to be protected by the Data Protection Act 2018.[1] Modern laws may need to adapt.[1]

Marks are indicative only. Refer to the band descriptions and levels of response guidance for extended response questions on page 101.

LEGISLATION

There are three main areas of **legislation** to understand in relation to Computer Science:

- Data Protection Act 2018
- Computer Misuse Act 1990
- Copyright, Designs and Patents Act 1988

Data Protection Act 2018

The **Data Protection Act** was updated in 2018 to incorporate the General Data Protection Regulations (GDPR). It has six principles that govern how data should be stored and processed.

These state that data must be:

1. Fairly and lawfully processed
2. Used for specific purposes only
3. Adequate, relevant and not excessive
4. Accurate and up-to-date
5. Not be kept longer than necessary
6. Kept secure

In addition, the data must be kept in accordance with the rights of data subjects.

Computer Misuse Act 1990

The **Computer Misuse Act** was introduced in 1990 to make unauthorised access to programs or data (hacking) and cybercrime illegal. The act recognises three offences:

1. Unauthorised access to computer material.
2. Unauthorised access with intent to commit or facilitate a crime.
3. Unauthorised modification of computer material.

It is also illegal to make, supply or obtain anything which can be used in computer misuse offences, including the production and distribution of malware.

Copyright, Designs and Patents Act 1988

This act is designed to protect the works of companies and individuals from being illegally used, copied or distributed. 'Works' include books, music, images, video and software.

EXAMINATION PRACTICE

1. Businesses commonly have a policy of replacing their computer hardware and equipment every three years.

   Discuss the environmental impacts of replacing working hardware and equipment so regularly.   [6]

2. WhatsApp is a free text and voice messaging application which allows users to message each other using a mobile or desktop device. It uses end-to-end encryption between sender and recipient.
   (a) Explain the advantage to users of end-to-end encryption.   [2]
   (b) Explain the possible threats to national security of end-to-end encryption.   [2]

3. Implanting computer-based chips in humans is likely to become more common in future.

   Describe **two** potential applications for computer-based implants. For each application, give **one** advantage and **one** disadvantage to the wearer.

   Application 1:   [1]
       Advantage: [1]
       Disadvantage: [1]

   Application 2:   [1]
       Advantage: [1]
       Disadvantage: [1]

4. The world has seen a surge in the number of people and companies working remotely.

   Discuss the reasons for this growth, and the legal and ethical impacts of this trend.
   Consider cloud storage, cyber security and mobile technologies in your answer.   [6]

5. Computer programs are being used in some countries to help a judge determine the sentence when a person is convicted of a criminal offence. The algorithm is designed to accept input data such as the offender's criminal history, family history, social life, economic stability and opinions and assess the risk of the person reoffending.

   Discuss the benefits, risks and ethical implications of using computer programs in this context.   [6]

EXAMINATION PRACTICE ANSWERS

1. (a) 13 (the number of items in the list) [1]
   (b) 3 6 7 [3]
   (c) 9 found at position 3 (item 9 is the 4th in the list, counting from 0) [1]
   (d) It performs a linear search on the list for an item entered by the user. If the item is not found, it prints "Invalid number". [2]

   Download the program solutions in Python from www.pgonline.co.uk

2. (a) It acts as a 'flag' which is set to False when a pass through the list is made and no items are swapped, meaning that the list is now sorted. [2]
   (b) temp ← names[n]
       names[n] ← names[n+1]
       names[n+1] ← temp [3]
   (c) Adam Edna Charlie Jack Ken Maria Victor
       Adam Charlie Edna Jack Ken Maria Victor [2]
   (d) 3 passes. Swaps are made on the first two passes. The list will be sorted after the second pass, and on the third pass, no swaps are made, so swapMade is set to False and the while loop terminates. [2]

3. (a) Algorithm design [1]
   (b) Decomposition [1]
   (c) Abstraction [1]

4. (a) [4]

num	a	b	ans
	0	0	0
3	3	1	0
8	11	2	0
2	13	3	0
5	18	4	0
−1			4.5

   (b) It calculates the average of the numbers input by the user. [1]

1. (a) String   (b) Boolean   (c) integer   (d) real/float [4]

2. (a) line 02 [1]
   (b) Should be: `height = float(input())` [2]
   (c) Line 03 [1]
   (d) `if height < 1.2:` [1]

3. (a) True [1]
   (b) 1 [1]
   (c) 5 [1]

4. (a) `not("7" in str(count))` (***Tip:*** *Convert the integer 7 and the integer count to strings. Outer brackets are optional.*) [3]
   (b) `for count in range(1,101):`
       `    if not("7" in str(count)) and not(count % 5 == 0):`
       `        print(count)`
       or, `if not("7" in str(count)) and (count % 5 != 0):`
       or, `if not("7" in str(count) or (count % 5 == 0)):` [3]

5.
```
mark = int(input("Please enter mark: "))
if mark >= 80:
    print(mark, "Distinction")
elif mark >= 65:
    print(mark, "Merit")
elif mark >= 50:
    print(mark, "Pass")
else:
    print(mark, "Fail")
```
[6]

   (Tip: First test for mark >=80. A mark >= 80 is also >= 50. Alternative conditions acceptable.)

6. (a)
```
for n in range(6):
    print(name[n])
```
[2]

   (Tip: remember that the first element of the array is name[0]. n in range(6) means n goes from 0 to 5.)

   (b) A linear search because as there are only 6 names, the execution time difference will be negligible and it is much simpler to code than a binary search. Or, a binary search as the list is sorted and may grow in length. [2]

7. (a) `results[3][2]` [1]

   (b)
```
for row in range(5):
    wins = wins + results[row][0]
    draws = draws + results[row][1]
    losses = losses + results[row][2]
print(wins, draws, losses)
```
[5]

8. (a) MAGRE290212 [1]
   (b)
```
surname = "BULLINGDEN"
dob = "120509"
username = firstname[0:2] + surname[0:3] + dob
```
[4]

9. (a) line 09 [1]
   (b) line 05 [1]
   (c) The input statement displays a prompt for the user and accepts input. The input is converted to an integer and assigned to the variable **throws**. [3]
   (d) A random number between 1 and 6 is generated by the function random()and assigned to the variable **throw1**. [2]
   (e) **equalThrows**, **equal**, or something similar. [1]
   (f) 3 1 (Do not allow comma after 3.) [2]

10. The **email address** could be validated to ensure it contains the characters "@" and "." (Format check.)
    Password could be checked against the password held on file to ensure it matches. (Lookup check.)
    Date of birth could be checked to ensure it is a valid date, between 18 and 100 years before current date (assuming 18 is the youngest age at which a customer can register). (**Range check**.)
    Format check could be carried out on postcode to ensure that it is a valid format. (Any 3 answers.) [6]

11. (a)
```
tableToPrint = int(input("Enter table that you wish to print: "))
timesTable(tableToPrint)
```
[4]
    (b) n, xTimesN [1]
    (c) `str()` converts an integer (or a floating point number) to a string. `range()` returns a sequence of numbers. [2]

12. (a)
```
02   x = a * a          # or x = a ** 2
03   y = b * b + c * c  # or y = b ** 2 + c ** 2
```
[2]
    (b)
```
if triangle(sideA, sideB, sideC):
    print("Right-angled")
else:
    print("Not right-angled")
```
[3]
    or, with alternative answer:
```
    rtAngle = triangle(sideA, sideB, sideC)
    if rtAngle:
        ...
```

13. (a)

variable	variable type
savedPassword	string
validPassword	Boolean
attempts	integer

[3]

(b) `04  while not validPassword and attempts < 3:` [1]

(c) `07  validPassword == True` [1]

(d) `12  if validPassword == True` or `if not validPassword == False` [1]

(e) To prevent a hacker from trying out every possible or likely sequence of letters until they hit on the correct password.
So that if the user has simply forgotten their password they can automatically be taken to a "forgotten password" routine after 3 attempts. [3]

14. (a) (i) A logic error will not prevent the program from running but will produce an unexpected or erroneous output. [1]

(ii) `if bagCount >= 1 and bagCount <=4 then` [1]

(b) Line 01 should be written: `bagCount = int(input("Enter number of bags"))`

(c) [5]

No.	Test purpose	Test data	Actual outcome
1	Check lowest valid boundary	0	Input is accepted
2	Check highest valid boundary	4	Input is accepted
3	Check invalid boundary data	-1, 5	Error message "Invalid bag allowance" is displayed
4	Check valid entry	2	Input is accepted
5	Check erroneous entry	*! (Any non-numeric character)	Program will crash

15. Algorithm 1 will take more time to execute, which is especially inefficient for a large number range, as it has to perform the FOR loop many times (e.g. 10,000 times to add numbers 1–10,000). Algorithm 2 solves the problem by executing just one statement to perform the calculation. [3]

16. Subroutines can be tested separately
Once proved correct, subroutines can be saved in a library and used in different programs
Subroutines can be called many times in the same program
Maintenance of programs using tested, well-documented subroutines is easier [3]

Section 3

1. (a) 4,500 bytes [1]

(b) 2,000 MB [1]

(c) (i) 00011100 [1]

(ii) Shifting one place right results in 00111010. This is the same result as dividing by 2. The leftmost bit is filled with 0 when the number is shifted right. [2]

2. (a) The set of characters or symbols that a computer can display using a particular representation, e.g. ASCII or Unicode. [1]

(b) 320 bytes. [1]

(c) (i) 1110, 1000. [2]

(ii) Unicode uses more bytes (2 per character), which enables more characters from different languages (e.g. Greek, Russian, Chinese) to be represented. [2]

3. (a) [3]

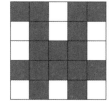

(b) 20 11 20 [1]

(c) Lossy compression (JPG) would provide the smallest file size whilst maintaining a good quality image. Whilst some data is lost during the compression process, the image would still be recognisable. The smaller file size would mean it was able to download and display on a browser more quickly. Lossy compression (PNG) may be most suitable if background transparency is required. A GIF image is a lossless format with a limited colour depth which would minimise the time taken to download and display the image. GIFs also handle simple animations and transparent pixels. [4]

4. (a) Sample resolution means the number of bits allocated to each recorded sample. [1]

(b) The greater the number of bits, the more accurately the wave height of each sample can be recorded. This increases the overall quality of the recording as it will create a closer representation of the original sound. [2]

(c) Sampling rate is the number of samples taken each second. As the sampling rate is increased, the file size will increase as each sample is saved at the given sample resolution. [2]

5. Huffman coding assesses the frequency of each letter in a large document or block of text. From the frequencies, a tree is formed. Those with the highest frequencies appear nearer the top of the tree and will have the shortest binary codes to represent them. A binary code is assigned to each character that appears in the text, including spaces. The code is worked out by tracing through the tree where a 0 means take the left branch and a 1 means take the right branch.
(Accept L/R as 1/0 or 0/1.) [4]

Section 4

1. (a) [2]

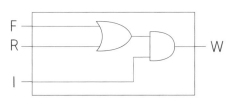

(b) One mark for each pair of correct results at output W. [4]

Front tyre pressure low (F)	Rear tyre pressure low (R)	Ignition on (I)	Working space F OR R	Warning light on (W)
0	0	0	0	0
0	0	1	0	0
0	1	0	1	0
0	1	1	1	1
1	0	0	1	0
1	0	1	1	1
1	1	0	1	0
1	1	1	1	1

2. (a) (A AND B) XOR ((NOT B) OR C) or using notation as $X = (A \cdot B) \oplus (\overline{B} + C)$ [3]

(b) X = 0 [1]

3. (a) The OS controls user access to prevent one user from accessing files or folders they should not have access to. / Security updates from software manufacturers and are also downloaded to help fix bugs and improve security against malware. /Files on the hard disk may also be encrypted. [2]

(b) Input / output (peripheral) device management, application management, memory management. [3]

4. B. Compression software [1]

5. D. The programs are stored in ROM [1]

6. A high-level language is written in an English-like syntax. A low-level language such as assembly code uses mnemonics to code instructions.
A high-level language is not particular to any type of hardware so can be used on any system. A low-level language is specific to a particular computer architecture.
High-level code must be translated into machine code by a compiler or interpreter before it can be executed. Assembly code is translated by an assembler and this is a much simpler process since each assembly code statement generally translates into one machine code instruction. (Any 2 points for each language type.) [4]

7. A compiler translates the whole program (source code) into object code which can then be saved and executed whenever required without recompiling. If there are any syntax errors in the program, they are reported to the programmer and the compilation fails.

An interpreter translates each line and then executes it if it is free of syntax errors. Otherwise, it highlights the syntax error and stops interpreting. No object code is produced so the program must be interpreted before execution each time. A compiled program will generally execute faster. [4]

8. (a) The control unit controls data moving through the CPU, by timing operations within the CPU. It decodes instructions, and sends and receives control signals to input, output and storage devices. [2]

(b) The ALU carries out arithmetic operations such as adding two numbers, and logical operations such as AND, OR and NOT. It also carries out shift operations. [2]

9. (a) Cache memory is faster than RAM so instructions and data can be accessed more quickly than data and instructions held in RAM. [2]

(b) Cache is more expensive than RAM. [1]

10. One CPU may have more cache memory than the other. One CPU may have multiple cores, which will increase performance as several instructions can be carried out simultaneously. Disk access speed will affect speed when reading or writing data, and different components, e.g. SSD or HDD will affect speed. Different architectures, for example PCs and smartphones cannot be compared by clock speed and will perform differently at same clock speed. A computer with more RAM will operate faster under some circumstances as it will make less use of virtual memory, which slows down the execution of programs. [4]

11. For a computer's boot-up instructions / BIOS, or to hold the program in an embedded device. [1]

12. SSD. An SSD is lightweight and unaffected by knocks or bumps as it has no moving parts. It runs with less power, increasing the battery life of the tablet. It produces less heat when running so a fan is not required, saving space and weight inside the tablet.[3]

13. Arc Accounts will save money on in-house server maintenance staff and hardware replacements since this will be taken care of by the Cloud storage provider. Service and security will also be taken care of but ArcAccounts will still be responsible for any security breaches or loss of data. They will need to consider the legal position in those cases and whether they want to lose that level of control over their own data. The potential costs of Cloud storage will increase as the volume of data stored increases, but this allows for the company to grow without upgrading their own infrastructure. Staff may be able to access data from any computer in the world with an Internet connection so they can expand their company internationally. ArcAccounts will need a very reliable and fast Internet connection to ensure that access is always available. This may need to be upgraded if they do not currently have good bandwidth. (Refer to the mark band descriptors on page 101.) [6]

14. A hard disk drive stores data as magnetised particles on concentric tracks on one or more platters. The particles have either north or south polarity representing 1 or 0. The platter is divided into sectors. A read/write head moves across the disk platter to the correct location. When not in use, the head is parked. [4]

Section 5

1. (a) Peripherals such as printers and scanners may be shared. Internet connections may be shared. Files can be stored and backed up on a central server and may be accessed from any computer in the network. Software can be installed centrally rather than on every machine separately. [3]

(b) Marks awarded for labelled server, labelled switch or hub, terminals, single cable to each terminal; from the switch. [3]

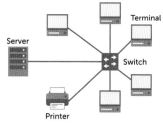

(c) Ethernet cable; fibre optic cable. [1]

(d) Facial/fingerprint/voice recognition. The user looks at a camera/touches a sensor/speaks into a microphone. The computer scans the face/fingerprint/analyses the voice pattern and compares it with previously captured and stored images/prints/recording analysis. If they match, the user is authenticated. A PIN or username and password can be entered. If they match previously stored entries for that user, access is granted. Shape recognition asks a user to draw a pattern on the screen. If this pattern matches a pattern pre-recorded by the user, access is permitted. [3]

(e) Encryption. [1]

(f) An algorithm is used with an encryption key to encrypt data by the sender into ciphertext. The recipient computer uses their key to decrypt or decipher the text back into plaintext. [2]

2. A LAN connects devices within one site or location; a WAN links more than one remote geographical location to another. LANs are typically created using hardware and connections owned by a single person or organisation; WANs usually use a shared infrastructure under shared ownership / use third party connections such as phone lines and satellite connections; Data transmission speed is likely to be higher across a LAN than across a WAN. Encryption is more likely to be used with a WAN as it is more likely to be public. A LAN is more likely to be private and may not need encryption. LAN connections can be more reliably managed as they are under local control by network administrators; WAN connections can suffer under heavy traffic, viruses, weather or physical damage outside the control of local administrators or users. [4]

3. (a) Personal Area Network (PAN). [1]
   (b) Bluetooth can create its own private network that can be connected to within roughly 10m. A Wi-Fi connection is unlikely to be available in many travel locations and would require setting up the speaker device and others on the Wi-Fi network with the permission of the network owner. A wired connection would remove the freedom of the user to move around with their mobile phone whilst remaining connected. [3]

4. (a) Hypertext Transfer Protocol (HTTP); Hypertext Transfer Protocol Secure HTTPS. [1]
   (b) A protocol is a common set of rules which everything must follow for things to function without error. Without a protocol, there would be no way to ensure that every browser could access every web server using the same methods. The World Wide Web would fail to operate. [2]
   (c) (i) Application layer. [1]
       (ii) The Transport layer establishes/sets up the connection between sending and recipient computers. It divides data into packets, numbers packets and adds a port number. Then it reassembles packets into order once received, handles missing packet errors and resends replacement packets. [3]

5. [4]

Issue	Protection method
Internal hacker illegally accessing files and changing or deleting data on a LAN	Firewall
Hackers attempting to access to ports on a server which are not in use	Encryption
Users attempting to connect to a Wi-Fi access point they are disallowed from using	MAC address filtering
Confidential data transmitted over the Internet being read	User authentication

Section 6

1. (a) Social engineering is the dishonest manipulation of people to cause them to divulge data or information against their (or their company's) better judgement. [2]
   (b) (i) Customers may have their data stolen which can be used to steal their identity. This may impact the access they have to their bank account and could result in unauthorised withdrawals. [1]
       (ii) Staff may require further training on how to handle and identify such attacks. They may cause a liability for the bank to repay any money that has been fraudulently withdrawn. They may be formally cautioned with regard to their job. [1]

2. External drives or USB storage devices may be infected with a virus and used with computers in the office. These must be checked for viruses using up-to-date antivirus software before use. Downloading email content or files from unknown senders or websites may contain infected files. Anti-malware software and a policy to prevent the use of external drives would lessen the risk of both dangers. Using out of date applications or anti-malware software could allow hackers or threats to access her system through known security holes. Updating her systems and application software with patches and downloading the latest anti-malware software will close these holes. Up-to-date virus checkers will be able to find the most recent threats. [4]

3. (a) The purpose of penetration testing is to detect weaknesses in an organisation's computer security systems, so that they can be fixed. [2]
   (b) 'White box' penetration testing involves sharing full network and system information with the tester. A "white hat" hacker is employed to put themselves in the position of a dishonest employee to see if they can find a weakness in the security system and gain entry to parts of the system and data which they are not authorised to view or change. Any weakness is then reported, and extra security measures put in place to fix the vulnerability. [3]

4. (a) Poorly written or punctuated email. Links that reveal a fake website address when you hover over them that do not link you to where you might expect. An element of urgency expressed in the email, for example "click to win now", or a plea for funds to help someone in need. Email not addressed to you personally. [3]
   (b) Installation of ransomware, malware or keylogger software when a link is clicked. Divulgence of personal details such as passwords, or bank information, leading to data loss, identity theft or financial loss. [2]

5.

Description	Letter
Malware that automatically replicates itself on a computer.	C
A cyber attack design to redirect legitimate website traffic to a fake website.	A
Use of human features for authentication.	D

[3]

Section 7

1.

Description	Letter
A column of data	B
Uniquely identifies a row of data in a database	C
A link between two tables	E

[3]

2. (a) 4 [1]
   (b) Event.holderID [1]
   (c) Holder data is not duplicated when the same record holder earns a second record. If all the data was held in a single table, all the data about the record holder would have to be entered twice. (Data redundancy). This could also lead to data inconsistency, if the two instances of the same data were not entered in exactly the same way. E.g. a name could be misspelt in one entry. One instance may be updated or deleted without updating the other. This would create inconsistent or conflicting data. [4]
   (d) SELECT firstname, surname, nationality [4]
   FROM Holder
   WHERE nationality = 'American'
   ORDER BY surname ASC
   (e) (i) SELECT surname, title, speed
   FROM Holder, Event
   WHERE (year > '2015') AND (Holder.holderID = Event.holderID)
   ORDER BY year DESC [4]
   (ii) [2]

surname	title	speed
Shutkever	Fastest burrito eaten	35.26s
Ohler	Fastest mobility scooter	180 kmh

   (f) To change the speed value for the fastest mobility scooter / record with eventID 2 from 180 kmh to 182.4 kmh. [2]
   (g) DELETE FROM Holder
   WHERE ID = 'WRH1034' [2]

Section 8

1. The volume of e-waste is increased. Working equipment is sometimes unnecessarily sent to landfill in the UK, and also sent abroad to be disposed of. This is a waste of resources, especially rare raw materials used in the latest technology that must be mined to be replaced. Mining causes significant environmental damage and some metals are already in short supply.

   Toxic chemicals are used in the manufacture of hardware and can leak into the environment if left in landfill. Some nations receive our e-waste and extract valuable metals through burning equipment which pollutes the air, waterways and the land. Refer to the mark band descriptors on page 101. [6]

2. (a) Messages cannot be hacked while in transmission and are private. Only the sender and recipient can read it. [2]
   (b) Police and security services will not be able to access messages between known criminals or terrorists and may have less chance of preventing crime/terrorist attacks. [2]

3. Application: Medical implants e.g. heart pacemakers/implant to track wearer's vital signs such as heart rate / brain implants for Parkinson's sufferers. Advantage: Can be lifesaving. Disadvantage: Could be hacked and cause harm or death. [3]
   Application: Tracking implants e.g. to track military spies, or patients with severe dementia. Advantage: Safety, security and peace of mind. Disadvantage: Invasion of privacy, cannot be turned off by wearer. [3]
   Application: Cochlea implant. Advantage: Allows a person to hear. Disadvantage: Complications from the operation. [3]
   (Accept other valid answers.)

4. **Reasons:** Mobile technologies have become increasingly available and affordable for companies and individuals. Software companies are increasingly providing their services via the cloud, which is more cost-effective and more environmentally friendly than thousands of individual company servers. For individuals, cloud storage gives the convenience of automatic backup and access from anywhere with an Internet connection.

    Ethical issues:

    Employees may be trusted to work away from the office using mobile technologies. Some may abuse this trust while they are not being observed.

    Remote working facilities may create a divide between those employees and employers who are able to afford or have access to high-bandwidth connections and mobile technology to enable home working and those who cannot. This may limit the work that some people are able to apply for and may hinder the progress of some smaller less-well-funded companies.

    Legal issues:

    The company using cloud storage will still be responsible under the Data Protection Act for breaches of security regarding personal data. Sensitive data will also need to be encrypted for all transmissions between colleagues and between the main server.   [6]

    This question should be marked against the band descriptions and levels of response guidance for extended response questions on page 101.

5. The benefits are that a computer algorithm should eliminate any personal prejudices that a judge may hold, and it should be fair to all convicted offenders. The algorithm should improve on the accuracy of human decision makers by taking many more factors into account.

    However, the algorithms work in such a way that it is almost impossible to figure out how they reach a decision, so it is very difficult to challenge the sentence. The algorithms are typically written by private companies rather than government agencies. Whilst the programs can take away the possibility that a judge will be biased against people, the algorithms may themselves be programmed to have biases against particular characteristics.

    There are ethical concerns that the sentencing algorithm used may be biased and that the lack of transparency in how the decision is reached leads to unfair sentencing.   [6]

    This question should be marked against the band descriptions and levels of response guidance for extended response questions on page 101.

LEVELS OF RESPONSE GUIDANCE FOR EXTENDED RESPONSE QUESTIONS

Questions that require extended writing use mark bands. The whole answer will be marked together to determine which mark band it fits into and which mark should be awarded within the mark band.

Level	Description	Mark range
3	• Thoughts, explanations, descriptions and ideas are consistent throughout the response • Clear explanations or descriptions • Evidence and examples are given to support explanations and descriptions • Logically structured response • Both advantages and disadvantages considered if required • Points and examples included that are relevant to the question • Points discussed / explained • At least three points typically required	5–6 marks
2	• Logically structured response • Clear and accurate explanations or descriptions • Both advantages and disadvantages considered if required • At least two points typically required	3–4 marks
1	• A description of some points has been given • Advantages or disadvantages briefly considered if required • At least one point typically required	1–2 marks
0	• No answer has been given or the answer given is not worth any marks	0 marks

The above descriptors have been written in simple language to give an indication of the expectations of each mark band. See the AQA website at **www.aqa.org.uk** for the official mark schemes used.

INDEX

EXAMINATION TIPS

With your examination practice, apply a boundary approximation using the following table. Be aware that boundaries are usually a few percentage points either side of this.

Grade	9	8	7	6	5	4	3	2	1
Boundary	90%	80%	75%	65%	60%	50%	35%	25%	15%

1. Read each question very carefully as some students give answers to questions they think are appearing rather than the actual question.

2. In calculation questions, marks are often given for working. You should make sure to show your working in case you make a mistake and the answer is incorrect.

3. Algorithms can be given as pseudo-code or flowcharts unless the question explicitly states otherwise. If you make a mistake when drawing flowchart symbols, you are unlikely to be penalised unless you make the algorithm unclear.

4. Arrows coming out of decision symbols must be labelled to make an algorithm clear.

5. If you need to produce pseudo-code, then `string ← USERINPUT` will count as two statements – one for collecting user input and one for the assignment – this line of code may therefore be worth two marks.

6. You may be asked to explain why one algorithm is better than another – for example, sorting algorithms. 'Quicker' and 'faster' are not acceptable answers. You must explain why the algorithm is quicker or faster to gain a mark.

7. This is also the case in programming code. If a more efficient code change is made, it is not acceptable to describe the improvement as 'faster' or 'uses less storage' unless there is an explanation of why this is the case.

8. When drawing logic gate diagrams, students often use the incorrect symbols for gates.

9. If you are asked for an explanation of issues that affect an organisation, many students will give how they affect an individual rather than the organisation which limits the marks available. Again, care needs to be taken with reading the question closely.

10. When performing binary arithmetic, you can use any method you wish – for example, convert to decimal, perform the addition, then convert back, alternatively you can do the addition directly in binary which is often faster.
    The same applies for converting numbers between hexadecimal to binary where you can convert from hex to decimal and then to binary.

11. Common misconceptions about ROM are that it is usually used to store application software or that there is typically more ROM than RAM. Both of these are incorrect.

12. Be careful with vague answers. For cloud storage benefits it is not acceptable to write that it 'has more space' or 'costs less'. Correct answers would be that 'it allows access to a larger amount of storage capacity' or that 'it allows the purchase of a cheaper computer with less storage capacity'.

13. When giving the differences of WANs and LANs many responses will say that 'WANs are larger'. This isn't acceptable. You need to say that a WAN links one remote geographical site/location to another.

14. Many students, especially weaker ones, do not have their answers match the context of the question. Consider a travel agent that stores customer and business data electronically and needs to prevent infections from malware. Some students would mention keeping records on paper or disconnecting computers from the network. These would help to prevent infections but are not appropriate for the type of business and therefore are unlikely to be markworthy.

Good luck!